THE REVIVE CAFE COOKBOOK 3
www.revive.co.nz

Copyright © Revive Concepts Limited 2013
Published by Revive Concepts Limited
First printing 2013

ISBN 978-0-473-23594-9

Also by Jeremy Dixon:　The Revive Cafe Cookbook
　　　　　　　　　　　　The Revive Cafe Cookbook 2

All rights reserved. Except as provided under copyright law, no part of this book may be reproduced in any way without permission in writing from the publishers. "Revive" is a trademark of Revive Concepts Limited.

Produced in New Zealand
Food Preparation, Styling & Photography: Jeremy Dixon
Cafe Photography: Elesha Newton
Graphic Design: Rebecca Zwitser, Jeremy Dixon, Heather Cameron
Proof Reader: Nyree Tomkins
Recipe testing and proofing: Verity Dixon, Nyree Tomkins, Keryn McCutcheon, Kjirstnne Jensen, Elesha Newton, Narelle Liggett, Heather Cameron, Annelise Greenfield, Melinda Pullman, Mel Shaw, Dawn Simpson

The publisher makes no guarantee as to the availability of the products in this book. Every effort has been made to ensure the accuracy of the information presented and any claims made; however, it is the responsibility of the reader to ensure the suitability of the product and recipe for their particular needs. Many natural ingredients vary in size and texture, and differences in raw ingredients may marginally affect the outcome of some dishes. Most recipes have been adjusted from the cafe recipes to make them more appropriate for a home kitchen. All health advice given in this book is a guideline only. Professional medical or nutritional advice should be sought for any specific issues.

Metric and imperial measurements have been used in this cookbook. The tablespoon size used is 15ml (½fl oz), teaspoon 5ml (⅙fl oz) and cup 250ml (8fl oz). Some countries use slightly different sized measurements, however these will not make a significant difference to the outcome of the recipes.

Revive Cafes
24 Wyndham St, Auckland Central, New Zealand (previously located on Fort St)
33 Lorne St, Auckland Central, New Zealand

If you like the recipes in this book I recommend you sign up for my weekly inspirational Revive e-mails.
They contain a weekly recipe, cooking and lifestyle tips, the weekly Revive menu, special offers and Revive news.
Visit www.revive.co.nz to sign up or to purchase more copies of this or our other cookbooks online.
Privacy Policy: Revive will never share your details and you can unsubscribe at any time.
LIKE us on Facebook!　www.facebook.com/cafe.revive

Contents

Introduction 7
Cookbook Notes 8
Essentials 10
The 8 Keys to Healthy Living 12
Salads 15
Hotpots & Stir Fries 53
Main Meals 81
Soups 107
Flavour Boosters 121
Breakfasts 137
Sweet Things 153
Step-by-Step 177
Cookbook Series Reference Guide 188
Index 190

Introduction

In 2010 when I started thinking about writing a cookbook I phoned some publishers and received the same response from all of them. There were too many cookbooks, bookshops only wanted big name celebrity chefs and I should call them back in 5 years if I was interested and the market may have changed.

I decided that my unique healthy recipes had to be shared with the world and I was going to do it anyway. I took up photography, appointed a graphic designer and started assembling the components of what was to become my first cookbook!

In late 2011 I nervously placed the order for the printing of 4,000 of my first cookbook. The publishers told me that 1,000 was the average print run for a cafe, so I feared I would end up with a garage full of books for the next 20 years.

I never would have dreamed that two years later I would be on to the fifth printing of my first book, third printing of my second book and now finalising my third cookbook. It is great that people are keen to learn more about healthy cooking!

For this cookbook I have enlarged the sweets section, added a soup section (that was not included in the second book) and added a breakfast section.

All the recipes in this book are plant-based using whole foods that will enhance your life.

My mission in life is to help educate people to cook and eat healthier foods. The benefits of healthy eating just in terms of vitality and energy are significant, not to mention the lowered risks of developing life-long diseases.

I hope you will enjoy these recipes, learn some new skills and have life long great health!

Jeremy Dixon
August 2013

Cookbook Notes

Garlic, Ginger & Chilli

Garlic and ginger have amazing flavour enhancing properties and we use both extensively at Revive and in these recipes. Simply chop them up finely before adding to a dish or you can make your own purees by blending the garlic or ginger with a little oil. You can get pureed ginger from supermarkets.

I recommend that garlic should always be used fresh and never purchased in a puree as it has an unpleasant flavour. You can also buy pre-crushed/pureed chilli in a jar which is used in some recipes (in small amounts).

Sweeteners

The recipes do not use added refined sugar. The most convenient natural sweetener is liquid honey. Alternatively make up a batch of date puree (page 135) which is an excellent and inexpensive sweetener.

There are also other healthy sweeteners available such as apple sauce, agave and maple syrup, but these tend to be quite expensive for everyday use.

Oils

My favourite oil is rice bran oil and is what I use wherever "oil" is used. It is one of the best oils to cook with as it can withstand higher temperatures. Also, it has a very neutral taste so it is good for dressings.

Generally you should not heat olive oil. Grape seed and coconut oil are also good to use or you can use your favourite oil. In some recipes sesame oil is used and this is marked as such.

Beans/Chickpeas

I have used canned beans/chickpeas (garbanzo beans) in all of the recipes as this is the most convenient. Drain all cans before using.

If you can use freshly cooked beans they will taste better and are significantly cheaper. 1 can of beans is around 2 cups.

I recommend that you soak and cook your own beans and store them in your freezer. You will need to soak overnight in plenty of water (they expand three times their volume). Then cook in fresh water until soft, which will be between 30 minutes and 2 hours, depending on the bean and its age. Then freeze them in small containers for easy use.

To defrost, simply run some hot water over them in a sieve or colander for 30 seconds.

Nuts

Nuts are used in many dishes at Revive and in this cookbook. Roasted nuts are usually used where they are presented whole (in salads or stir fries) so they hold their crunchiness and do not go soggy.

Raw nuts are generally used where they will be blended as they will give a creamier result. However, having the wrong sort of nut will not affect the outcome of most recipes as they are usually interchangeable. You can use nut pieces if you want to minimise cost.

Where cashews or almonds are used to make a cream or milk, you can substitute sunflower seeds for a nut free version.

Creams
Different methods are used to make some dishes creamy. Coconut cream, almond cream and cashew cream can usually be used interchangeably.

Cooking Grains
I recommend that you cook extra grains like rice and quinoa and store in your refrigerator for an easy ingredient to use in the following few days. When you cook grains remember to use boiling water to save time, and first bring the grain to the boil before turning down to a simmer. Do not stir while cooking and keep the lid on.

Cooking Terms
Saute: to cook food on a high heat and in a little oil while stirring with a wooden spoon.
Simmer: to have food cooking at a low heat setting so it is just bubbling.
Roast: to bake in the oven covered with a little oil. Use fan bake setting to achieve more even cooking.

Mixing
You can mix most recipes in the pot you are cooking in or in a big mixing bowl. When mixing, stir gently so as not to damage the food. With salads, mix with your hands if possible. Gently lift up the ingredients and let them fall down with gravity rather than squeezing.

Peeling Vegetables
If in good clean condition, I do not peel potatoes, carrots or kumara. You gain extra vitamins, higher yield and save plenty of time.

Taste Test
It is difficult to get a recipe that works 100% the same every time, especially when you are using natural and fresh ingredients. Sizes in vegetables vary, spices and herbs differ in strength and you can even get differences in evaporation rates with different sized pots.

Make sure you taste test every dish before you serve and be willing to add more seasoning or a little more cooking time if necessary.

Blenders
Some recipes require a food processor (usually with an S blade). Other recipes require a blender or liquidiser (usually a tall jug with 4 pronged blades) or stick blender.

Some hotpots require a stick blender to blend the mixture to make it smoother and more consistent, but if you don't have one don't worry as this will not alter the outcome significantly.

Quantities
The quantities for each dish are an estimate and will vary depending on cooking times and ingredient size. I have used one cup as an average serving size.

Gluten Free & Dairy Free
A large proportion of the recipes are gluten free and/or dairy free. If you have any allergies you will need to check that each recipe is suitable and make adjustments as required.

Essentials Fridge & Freezer

Freeze and refrigerate leftovers and cooked grains/beans. Regularly stock up basic produce as required and as in season.

Freezer

- berries: boysenberries, blueberries, strawberries, raspberries
- cooked beans: chickpeas (garbanzo), red kidney, white, black, black-eye
- corn kernels
- peas
- red capsicum (bell peppers) diced
- spinach (usually in balls)

Refrigerator

- aioli (page 134)
- almond butter (page 133)
- basil pesto (page 135)
- crushed chilli (puree)
- date puree (page 135)
- ginger puree
- hummus or other dips
- leftover rice or quinoa
- relish
- soy sauce
- sweet chilli sauce
- Thai curry pastes: red, green, yellow, Massaman, Penang

Produce

- beetroot
- broccoli
- cabbage: red, white
- carrots
- cauliflower
- celery
- cucumber, telegraph
- fruit: bananas, lemons, apples
- garlic
- herbs: mint, parsley, basil, coriander (cilantro)
- kumara (sweet potato): red, orange, gold
- leeks
- lettuce: cos (romaine), iceberg, fancy, mesclun
- mesclun lettuce
- mushrooms
- onions: brown, red
- potatoes
- pumpkin
- silver beet (Swiss chard)
- spring onions (scallions)
- tomatoes
- zucchini (courgette)

Essentials Pantry

These items are shelf stable and generally have a long life. Always keep these stocked up so you can use at any time.

Herbs & Spices

coriander

cumin

curry powder

mixed herbs

smoked paprika

thyme

turmeric

General

canned chopped tomatoes

chickpea (besan/chana) flour

coconut cream

dried fruit: sultanas, raisins, prunes, dates, apricots

honey

oil: rice bran, olive, sesame

olives: kalamata, black

pasta and pasta sheets

peanut butter, tahini (sesame seed paste)

soy sauce or tamari

vinegar: balsamic, cider

whole-grain mustard

Grains

brown rice : long grain, short grain

bulghur wheat

couscous: fine, Israeli

quinoa

rolled oats: fine, jumbo

Beans

canned and dried beans: chickpeas (garbanzo), red kidney, white, black, black-eyed

dried lentils: red, yellow, brown (crimson), green

Nuts & Seeds

almonds

brazil nuts

cashew nuts

poppy seeds

sesame seeds: black, white

shredded coconut

sunflower seeds

The 8 Keys to Healthy Living

These are the health principles that Revive is founded on. It is not enough to just eat healthy food to have complete energy and vitality. There are other simple things that create good health, summarised by these 8 keys.

The good news is that if you apply these 8 simple steps in your day-to-day living, you will notice dramatic improvements in your vitality, health and quality of life.

1. Nutrition - eat plant-based foods, fresh produce and avoid processed foods and sugars.
2. Exercise - get at least 30 minutes every day.
3. Water - drink at least 2 litres (2 quarts) of pure water per day.
4. Sunshine - aim for 10 minutes minimum per day.
5. Temperance - free yourself from stimulants like alcohol, energy drinks, coffee and drugs.
6. Air - breathe deeply - start every day with 10 deep breaths.
7. Rest - get 8 hours quality sleep every night.
8. Trust - live at peace with everyone and your God.

Salads

Brown Rice Waldorf 16
Thai Ginger Slaw 18
Mega Cos Salad 20
Asian Ginger & Tofu Salad 22
Autumn Cauliflower Mingle 24
Blissful Sprout Medley 26
Rainbow Chickpeas 28
French Peanut Puy Lentils 30
Olivier, The Russian Salad 32
Sweet Shanghai Soy Beans 34
Tangy Leafy Salad 36
Italian Risotto 38
Apple Poppy Coleslaw 40
Caraway Kumara & Cabbage Salad 42
Basil Linguine Salad 44
Indian Curried Cauliflower & Chickpeas 46
Fragrant Thai Peanut Noodles 48
Quinoa & Cashew Mingle 50

This is one of the original salads at Revive that somehow was forgotten and not featured for many years. I rediscovered it in 2013 when I was hunting through some old files. It is a very fresh way to have brown rice. The apple and celery make a great crunchy combination.

Brown Rice Waldorf

MAKES 6 X 1 CUP SERVES

2 cups cooked long grain brown rice (1 cup uncooked)

1 cup celery chopped (around 1 large stalk)

2 cups red apple chopped into large cubes (around 1 large)

¼ cup parsley finely chopped

¼ cup aioli (page 134) or tofu mayo (page 132)

½ cup walnuts

½ cup sultanas

¾ teaspoon salt

1. Cook the rice or use leftover rice.
2. Chop the celery, apple and parsley.
3. In a bowl combine all ingredients.

If your sultanas are dry simply soak them in some boiling water for 5 minutes to plump them up. Make sure you drain the water!

This recipe is also great when you replace the sultanas with raisins, currants or cranberries.

Walnuts

These are a great crunchy nut to include in salads. They go rancid easily so make sure you buy fresh and store in your refrigerator.

This coleslaw is a staple at Revive and is on most weeks of the year. Many people find coleslaw boring, however just add some exciting flavours and you will love it. Raw cabbage is so good for you. The key when using cabbage is to use a combination of purple and white and other coloured vegetables so it looks appealing.

Thai Ginger Slaw

MAKES 6 X 1 CUP SERVES

3 cups red cabbage thinly sliced

2 cups white cabbage thinly sliced

2 cups carrots grated (around 1 large)

1 cup Thai ginger dressing (page 130)

1 cup mung bean sprouts

2 tablespoons black sesame seeds

½ cup coriander (cilantro) roughly chopped

1. Using a sharp knife or a food processor, slice the cabbage and grate the carrots.

2. Make the dressing.

3. In a bowl combine all ingredients together.

Reserve some of the colourful ingredients so you can add a garnish on top.

Mung Bean Sprouts

Mung bean sprouts come in short (young) or long (older) sizes. The longer ones add great texture and moistness to salads and work especially well in Asian style dishes.

Mega Cos Salad

MAKES 12 x 1 CUP SERVES

4 cups potatoes diced into 2cm (1in) cubes (around 3 potatoes)

1 tablespoon oil (for potatoes)

300g (10oz) pack tofu

1 tablespoon oil (for tofu)

½ teaspoon salt

4 cups cos (romaine) lettuce sliced into 1cm (½in) strips (around 1 small head)

2 cups tomatoes cubed (around 3 tomatoes)

2 cups broccoli florets lightly steamed and cooled in cold water (around 1 head)

10 stalks asparagus lightly steamed and cooled in cold water

1 can red kidney beans

½ cup aioli (page 134) or 1 cup tofu mayo (page 132)

½ teaspoon salt

optional: 2 tablespoons sweet chilli sauce

optional: ½ cup chopped fresh coriander (cilantro)

This is a great summer salad with lots of different ingredients. It is almost a meal in itself, and is very flexible so you can throw in any of your favourite beans or any vegetables you need to use up.

1. Combine the potatoes and oil in an oven tray and bake for 30 minutes at 180°C (350°F) or until soft and browned. Gently stir and mix half way through.

2. Dice the tofu into 1cm (½in) cubes and saute in a pan with oil and salt for around 10 minutes or until getting crispy.

3. Prepare the other ingredients, putting everything into a big mixing bowl.

4. Mix all ingredients together.

When you have cooked the green vegetables in water it is important to stop the cooking process by rinsing under cold water. This will also help retain their green colour.

If asparagus is not in season you can use sliced courgettes (zucchini) instead.

Roasting Vegetables

Roasted vegetables can make a salad really burst with flavour and texture. Simply cube your vegetables (the smaller they are the faster they cook) and coat with a little oil and salt and bake for between 20-40 minutes (depending on the vegetable and size).

Asian Ginger & Tofu Salad

MAKES 4 X 1 CUP SERVES

300g (10oz) firm tofu

1 tablespoon oil

¼ teaspoon salt

2 cups carrot cut into matchsticks (around 1 large carrot)

2 cups bok choy sliced into strips (around 2 heads)

½ red capsicum (bell pepper) cut into cubes

½ cup pickled ginger

2 tablespoons sesame oil

1 teaspoon white sesame seeds

1 teaspoon black sesame seeds

1. Chop the tofu into cubes.

2. In a pan saute the tofu and oil for around 5-10 minutes or until browned and firm on the outside. Toss regularly. When finished sprinkle the salt over it.

3. In a bowl combine all ingredients.

You can use any fresh leafy green vegetable with this salad.

Pickled Ginger

This is a Japanese ingredient often served with sushi and has a great tangy flavour. It is available from most Asian grocery stores. It sometimes comes with many preservatives and colourings so choose the brand carefully.

This is a lovely mingle of vegetables and beans and is very popular at Revive.

Autumn Cauliflower Mingle

MAKES 8 X 1 CUP SERVES

4 cups cauliflower cut into small florets

400g (12oz) can red kidney beans

100g (3oz) spinach roughly chopped (around 3 cups)

2 tablespoons sweet chilli sauce

½ teaspoon salt

¼ cup aioli (page 134) or tofu mayo (page 132)

1. Cook the cauliflower in boiling water for around 5 minutes or until just soft.
2. In a bowl combine all ingredients.
3. Serve warm or cold.

Don't overcook the cauliflower, it should still be firm to bite but not tasting raw.

Fresh Spinach

I often use spinach in salads where you would usually use lettuce or other leafy greens. Cut the tough stalks off and slice it. Do not add to warm or hot salads as it will wilt.

This is a great fresh and colourful salad and is unique in that it doesn't have a dressing. It is good served with other salads or meals. However if you want a dressing you can drizzle some olive oil and/or lemon juice over the top. It would also be awesome served with hummus or other dip.

Blissful Sprout Medley

MAKES 8 X 1 CUP SERVES

½ red capsicum (bell pepper) finely sliced

½ orange capsicum (bell pepper) finely sliced

½ yellow capsicum (bell pepper) finely sliced

125g (4oz) snow peas

1 cup mung bean sprouts (the short ones)

100g (3oz) baby spinach leaves

1 cup beetroot matchsticks (around 1 small beetroot)

1. Prepare all the vegetables.

2. If the beetroot is juicy, roughly dry with a paper towel. This will help stop it turning everything red.

3. In a bowl combine all ingredients.

When arranging make sure you drop the items gently onto the plate so they are heaped and the individual ingredients are evenly spread out.

If you prepare the vegetables ahead of time or need to store this salad, make sure it is covered and sprinkle some water through it to keep everything fresh.

Snow Peas/Sugar Snaps

These green additions are crunchy, fresh and add amazing texture to any salad. They come flat or round. When eaten, these peas have sweet skins that are soft enough to eat raw. You do want to cut off the stringy ends though.

The key to creating an appealing dish is to use a lot of contrasting colours - and capsicums are great at doing this. Using contrasting plate and bowl colours to serve also helps.

Rainbow Chickpeas

MAKES 6 X 1 CUP SERVES

1 cup celery diced (around 2 stalks)

1 cup carrots roughly diced (around 1 large carrot)

1 tablespoon finely chopped ginger or ginger puree

2 cloves garlic finely chopped or crushed

1 tablespoon oil

1 cup green beans halved

½ cup red onion diced

½ red capsicum (bell pepper) cubed

½ yellow capsicum (bell pepper) cubed

½ orange capsicum (bell pepper) cubed

400g (12oz) can chickpeas

½ teaspoon salt

½ cup fresh coriander (cilantro)

½ cup spring onions (scallions) sliced

1. In a large hot pan saute the celery, carrots, ginger, garlic and oil until they are starting to soften, around 4 minutes.

2. Optional: blanch the green beans into a pot of boiling water for 2 minutes which will take away the raw taste.

3. Add the beans, onion, capsicum and continue to cook for around 4 minutes or until soft.

4. Add the chickpeas and salt and keep warming.

5. Take off the heat and stir in the coriander and spring onions.

6. Serve warm or cold.

Err on the side of keeping the vegetables crunchy rather than soft.

You can also add nuts or seeds to this salad.

Coloured Capsicums

Also known as bell peppers. These are great when used with all of the colours - they create such a fresh, vibrant dish. Slice, dice, julienne, cube or whatever you favourite cut is!

French Peanut Puy Lentils

MAKES 5 X 1 CUP SERVES

¾ cup french speckled green (puy) lentils

5 cups boiling water

¼ cup aioli (page 134)

1 red capsicum (bell pepper) finely diced

1 green capsicum (bell pepper) finely diced

1 teaspoon salt

1 tablespoons sweet chilli sauce

½ cup peanuts

½ cup spring onions (scallions) sliced

½ cup celery finely diced (around 1 large stalk)

pinch cayenne pepper

1 tablespoon smoked paprika

garnish: spring onions (scallions)

1. Simmer lentils and water for around 30 minutes or until soft. It will yield around 2 cups of cooked lentils. Drain well.

2. In a bowl combine all ingredients.

3. Serve garnished with spring onions.

French Green (Puy) Lentils are best as they stick together when they are cooked. However you can use brown lentils but you need to be careful to cook them so they are soft but not starting to separate.

Cooking Lentils

Lentils are a great fast protein source. Just cook in plenty of water (usually 5 times the volume of lentils) until soft then drain off any remaining water. Red and yellow lentils can cook in under 15 minutes, where most other varieties take around 20-40 minutes.

An associate of mine, Theresa, lived in Russia for many years and recommended this salad to me. A Russian family's New Year's Eve celebration wouldn't be complete without this salad on the table. The same is true for weddings and pretty much any festive occasion. In fact, it is so closely linked to weddings that when a young couple begins to spend a lot of time together, friends and eager parents will ask them, "Is it time to prepare the Olivier?" Here is the Revive version of this salad.

Olivier, The Russian Salad

MAKES 7 X 1 CUP SERVES

4 cups potatoes diced 1cm (½in) (around 3 potatoes)

1 cup carrots finely diced (around 1 large carrot)

1 cup frozen peas

2 cups pickled gherkins finely diced

½ cup red onion finely diced (around half onion)

1 cup cucumber finely diced

1 teaspoon salt

½ cup aioli (page 134) or tofu mayo (page 132)

1 cup fresh herbs of your choice (coriander (cilantro), flat leaf parsley, dill, mint) roughly chopped

1. Bring a pot of water to boil. Add the potatoes and carrots. Cover and cook for around 10 minutes or until the potato is just soft. Drain and cool with cold water.

2. Combine all ingredients in a bowl.

Try to cut the vegetables approximately the same size.

If you are not serving straight away, mix everything except the dressing and mix in just before serving.

The frozen peas should not need cooking and will defrost quickly with the warm potato. If you are using cold potato you may need to put the peas in some hot water for a couple of minutes.

Pickled Gherkins

These are basically baby cucumbers. Make sure you get the "sour" ones not the sweet ones as they taste quite different. Chop them up and they add amazing bursts of flavour to a salad. Watch for flavour enhancers!

Sweet Shanghai Soy Beans

MAKES 4 X 1 CUP SERVES

1½ cups onion finely diced (around 1 medium onion)

2 cloves garlic finely chopped or crushed

1 teaspoon oil

400g (12oz) can soy beans (around 2 cups)

¼ cup pumpkin seeds

2 cups carrots cut into matchsticks (around 1 large carrot)

1 red capsicum (bell pepper) diced

3 tablespoons honey

1 tablespoon sesame oil

½ teaspoon salt

¼ cup coriander (cilantro) roughly chopped

1. In a pan saute the onion, garlic and oil for around 5 minutes or until clear.

2. Add remaining ingredients to the pan (except coriander) and cook for around 2 minutes. This is just to soften and lightly cook.

3. Stir the coriander through the salad and serve warm or cold.

Soy Beans

These are a great tasting bean not usually found in salads. You can buy them in cans or soak and cook like other beans. Make sure they are soft when you cook them.

This is a fresh salad that was born from random ingredients in my refrigerator one day when I needed a fresh salad to serve with a couple of hotpot dishes for some friends.

Tangy Leafy Salad

MAKES 6 X 1 CUP SERVES

2 cups red cabbage roughly sliced

2 cups spinach or bok choy roughly sliced

1 red capsicum (bell pepper) diced

½ telegraph cucumber (around 2 cups) diced

DRESSING:

1 tablespoon olive oil

2 tablespoons honey or date puree

¼ cup lemon juice

½ teaspoon salt

1. Combine all vegetable ingredients in a bowl.

2. Mix oil, honey, lemon juice and salt in a cup or shaker and gently mix through the salad.

For an even tangier salad, add 1 tablespoon of finely chopped ginger or ginger puree to the dressing.

SALADS 37

This is a good recipe to use with leftover rice and combines some very flavoursome Italian ingredients. Keep some leftover grains and fresh vegetables in your refrigerator and you can make meals like this easily in minutes.

Italian Risotto

MAKES 6 X 1 CUP SERVES

2 cups cooked short grain brown rice (1 cup uncooked)

1½ cups onion finely diced (around 1 onion)

2 cloves garlic finely chopped or crushed

1 tablespoon oil

100g (3oz) button mushrooms halved

1 yellow capsicum (bell pepper) cubed

½ cup sun-dried tomatoes sliced

½ cup olives

¼ cup parsley finely chopped

1. In a pot cook 1 cup rice with 2 cups of boiling water and simmer with the lid on for 25 minutes or until the water has disappeared.

2. In a hot pan saute the onion, garlic and oil until nearly clear (around 2-3 minutes).

3. Add the mushrooms and capsicum and cook for another 2-3 minutes or until soft.

4. Add remaining ingredients and rice. Toss around in the pan to lightly warm and mix.

5. Serve warm or cold.

You can either use sun-dried tomatoes in oil or buy them dried and just hydrate in boiling water.

Oil

Oil is important for cooking as it aids heat transfer, and helps stop sticking and burning. There are a lot of conflicting opinions on which oils to use, however the oils I prefer are rice bran, grape seed, coconut and olive oil. Oils are important to have in small quantities and are better than using animal fats like butter or heavily processed spreads like margarine.

SALADS 39

Apple Poppy Coleslaw

MAKES 6 X 1 CUP SERVES

2 cups white cabbage finely sliced

2 cups apples grated (around 2 apples)

1 cup spring onions (scallions)

½ red capsicum (bell pepper) diced

½ yellow capsicum (bell pepper) diced

½ cup mint finely sliced

¼ cup poppy seeds

DRESSING

¼ cup lemon juice

2 tablespoons oil

¼ teaspoon salt

1. Prepare the vegetables and combine all ingredients gently in a mixing bowl.

2. In a cup or shaker mix the dressing ingredients and mix through the vegetables.

Apple will go brown shortly after grating so make sure you mix the dressing with the apple as soon as you can.

Retain as much of the juice of the apple when grating and add it to the salad.

Knife Sharpening

It is great to have a sharp knife, however you need to keep it sharp. You can get a steel or stone and learn how to sharpen it. Ceramic water sharpeners are also great and so easy to use. The key is to sharpen a little each time you use it. Most knives will however require an expert to grind it every couple of years.

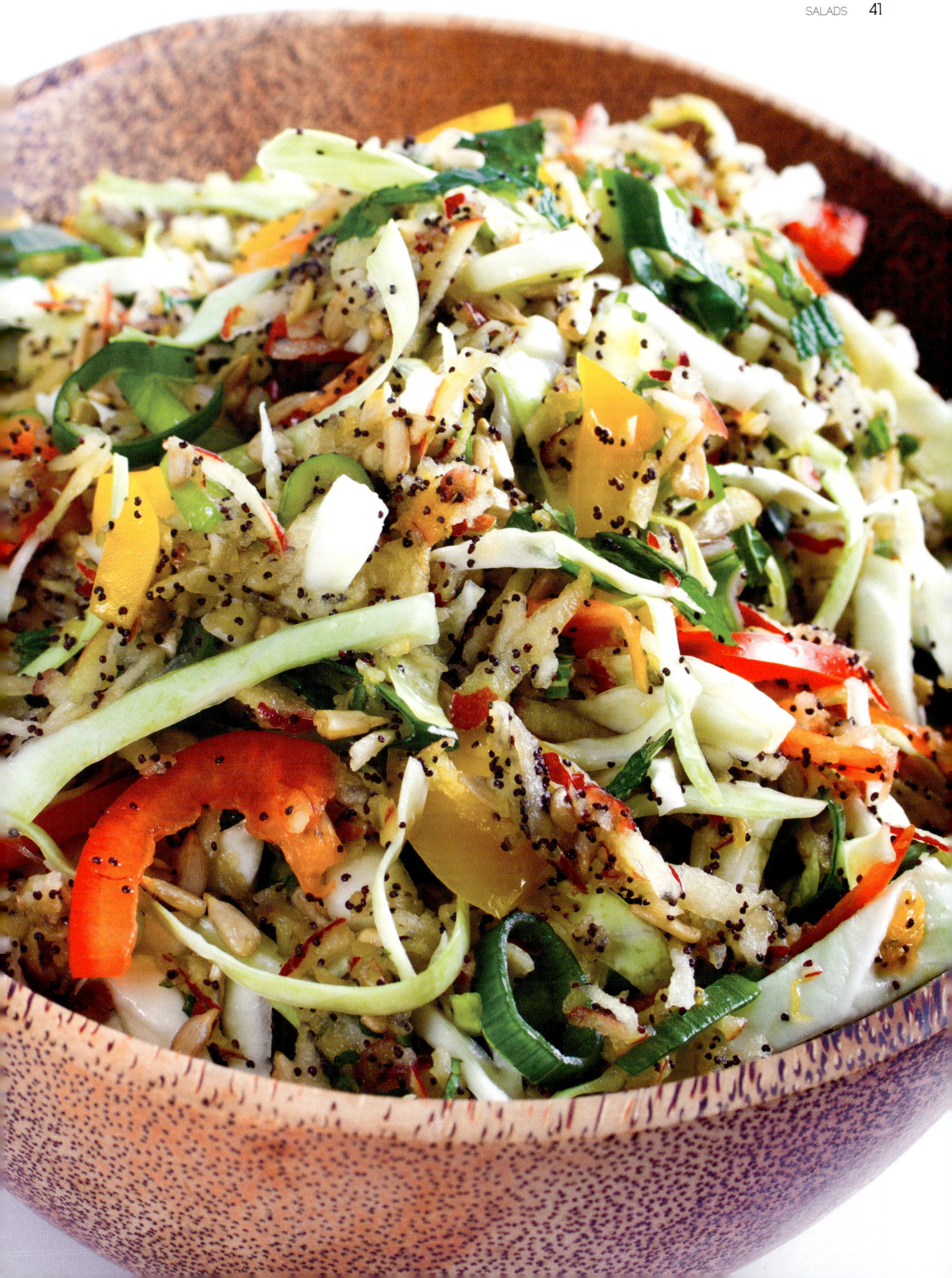

This can be used as a side dish or as a warm or cold salad. You cannot go wrong with kumara (sweet potato) it has such a lovely sweet taste.

Caraway Kumara & Cabbage Salad

MAKES 6 X 1 CUP SERVES

6 cups kumara (sweet potato) 2cm (1in) cubed (around 2 large)

2 tablespoons oil

1 tablespoon caraway seeds

4 cups white cabbage sliced

1 teaspoon salt

1. Combine the kumara and 1 tablespoon of oil in an oven tray and bake for 20 minutes at 180°C (350°F) or until soft and browned. Gently stir and mix half way through.

2. Saute the rest of the oil, caraway seeds and cabbage in a hot pan stirring regularly for around 3 minutes or until it is just soft. You want the cabbage to be slightly cooked but not wilted.

3. In a bowl combine all ingredients together.

4. Serve warm or cold.

If the kumara is clean and fresh I do not peel it. However if it is old and the skin is tough I will sometimes peel.

SALADS 43

This is a long-time favourite that we created in our first few months at Revive! The key is finding a good source of wholemeal pasta, we always found it hard to get a consistent supply. While we serve this dish as a salad, it can also be served as a main meal pasta dish when gently heated!

Basil Linguine Salad

MAKES 4 X 1 CUP SERVES

200g wholemeal linguine or fettuccine pasta

1 cup basil pesto (page 135)

½ red capsicum (bell pepper) thinly sliced

½ yellow capsicum (bell pepper) thinly sliced

½ cup black olives

garnish: cashew nuts

garnish: extra basil leaves

1. Cook the pasta according to the packet instructions. This is usually around 8 minutes in boiling water - however this will vary depending on the thickness.

2. In a bowl combine all the ingredients.

3. Serve warm or cold with cashew nuts and extra fresh basil leaves as a garnish.

This recipe uses the "plainer" black olives so as not to overpower the dish. However if you like really flavoursome olives try the Kalamata ones.

This recipe is also awesome with diced avocado!

Fettuccine/Linguine

You can buy nice wholemeal pastas from some supermarkets and whole foods stores. Cook to the packet directions and smother them with awesome flavours! Linguine is a narrower version of fettuccine.

SALADS 45

Indian Curried Cauliflower & Chickpeas

MAKES 8 X 1 CUP SERVES

2 cups cauliflower florets

400g (12oz) can chickpeas (garbanzo beans) (around 2 cups)

¼ cup fresh coriander (cilantro)

½ cup aioli (page 134) or tofu mayo (page 132)

½ cup red onions finely sliced (around ½ onion)

1 red capsicum (bell pepper) cubed

1 teaspoon curry powder

¼ teaspoon turmeric powder

3 tablespoons honey

1 teaspoon chilli puree

1 tablespoon lemon juice

1 teaspoon salt

50g (2oz) baby spinach leaves (around 2 cups)

1. Cook the cauliflower in boiling water for around 5 minutes or until just soft.
2. In a bowl combine all ingredients except spinach.
3. Mix in the spinach last so it does not get damaged.

While this recipe uses canned chickpeas, remember they taste amazing when you cook them yourself. Soak overnight, cook for around 30-60 minutes and store them in your freezer. Just run hot water over the chickpeas and they will defrost in under a minute.

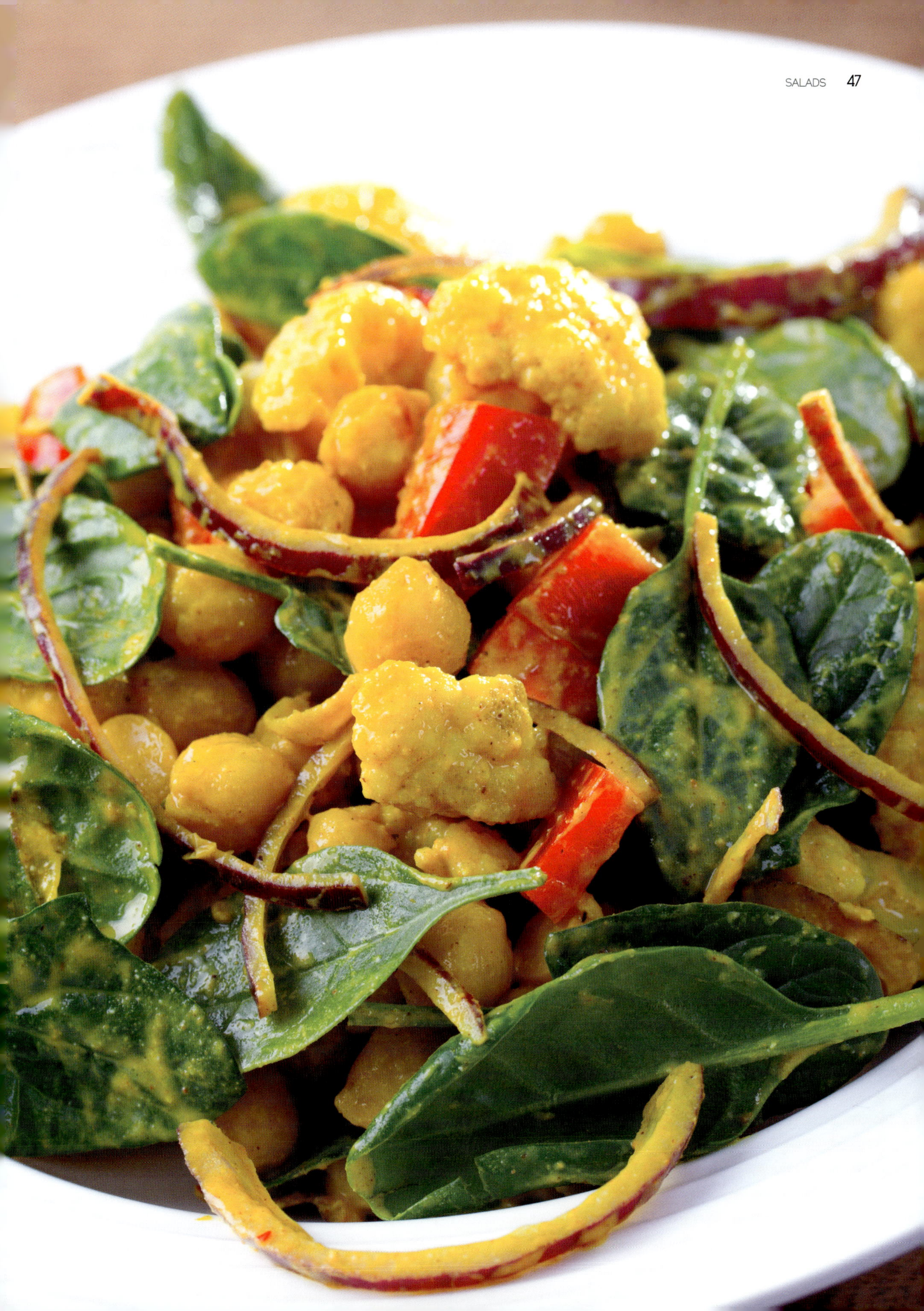

Fragrant Thai Peanut Noodles

I always find recipes similar to this in recipe books but they always include seafood and other fishy ingredients. So I created this version. It is not traditional Thai, but uses fresh ingredients with fresh Thai flavours. This recipe is so much fun as you just keep throwing ingredients into your food processor.

MAKES 6 LARGE SERVES

- 150g (5oz) rice noodles
- 4 litres (4 quarts) boiling water
- ½ cup radishes sliced (around 5)
- 2 cups carrots sliced (around 1 large carrots)
- 2 cups white cabbage sliced
- 1 cup telegraph cucumber sliced (around ¼)
- 3 tablespoons sesame seeds
- 1 cup peanuts
- 1 tablespoon sesame oil

DRESSING:

- 2 cloves garlic
- 2 tablespoons finely chopped ginger or ginger puree
- 200g (6oz) canned chopped tomatoes (½ can)
- ¼ teaspoon chilli puree
- 1 cup fresh coriander (cilantro)
- 2 tablespoons honey or date puree
- 2 tablespoons sesame oil
- ¼ cup lime juice (around 2-3 limes)
- garnish: coriander (cilantro)
- garnish: whole limes to squeeze over

1. Put the rice noodles in a mixing bowl and pour over the boiling water. Cover and let sit for around 10-20 minutes or until soft.

2. Put the dressing ingredients into a food processor and blend to make a fragrant sauce.

3. Change to a slicer blade (the thinnest one you have) and slice all the vegetables into the dressing.

4. In a pan lightly saute the sesame seeds, peanuts and oil.

5. Mix the dressing, vegetables and noodles together with your hands. Serve warm, garnished with the nut and seed mix, coriander and some lime juice.

If you do not own a food processor you can crush and mix the dressing and hand chop the vegetables.

Lime Juice

A squeeze of lime juice in many meals or salads can add an amazing bursting tangy flavour! Also great in iced water.

SALADS 49

I was deciding whether this recipe should be in the salads or hotpot section. It can be both. Quinoa salads are really popular in our salad bar. The ideal protein, it is soft and mingles well with many vegetables and flavours!

Quinoa & Cashew Mingle

MAKES 7 X 1 CUP SERVES

1 cup quinoa

2 cups boiling water

1½ cups onions finely diced (around 1 onion)

2 cloves garlic finely chopped or crushed

1 tablespoon oil

1 red capsicum (bell pepper) diced

2 cups courgettes (zucchini) randomly cut (around 2 courgettes)

2 cups carrots cut into matchsticks (around 1 large carrot)

½ cup cashew nuts raw

½ teaspoon ground turmeric

1 tablespoon honey or date puree

1 cup frozen peas

1. In a pot add the quinoa and water and bring back to the boil. Put the lid on and simmer on a low heat for around 12 minutes or until the water has disappeared.

2. In a pan or wok saute the onion, garlic and oil until the onion is clear.

3. Add the capsicum, courgette, carrots and cashews and fry for around 5 minutes or until they are just getting soft.

4. Add the remaining ingredients and heat until everything is heated through.

Capsicum and courgettes are mainly summer vegetables so in winter you can substitute other vegetables or use frozen vegetables.

Wooden Bowls

I love serving food in wooden bowls, they are great to have on hand and make food look fantastic. You can get lovely ones from the international trade stores or when you are travelling!

SALADS 51

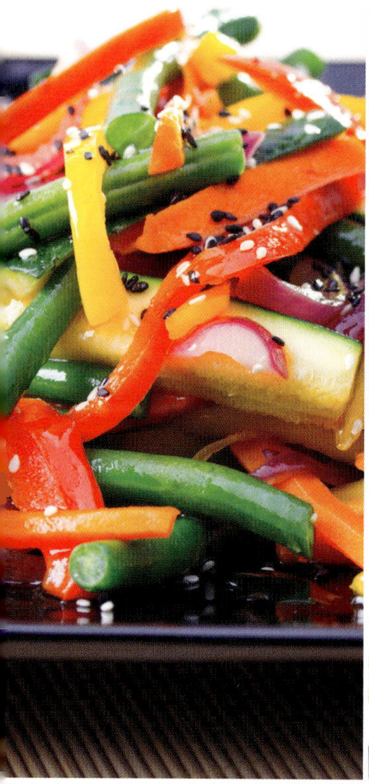
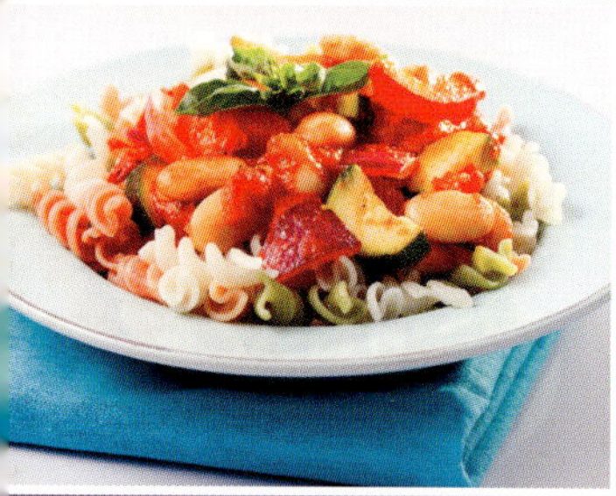
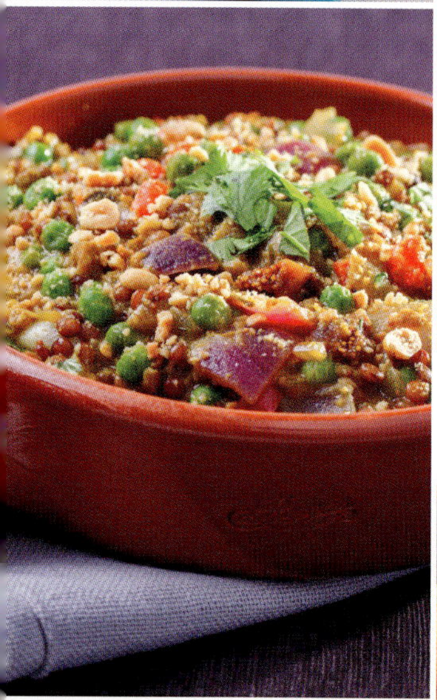
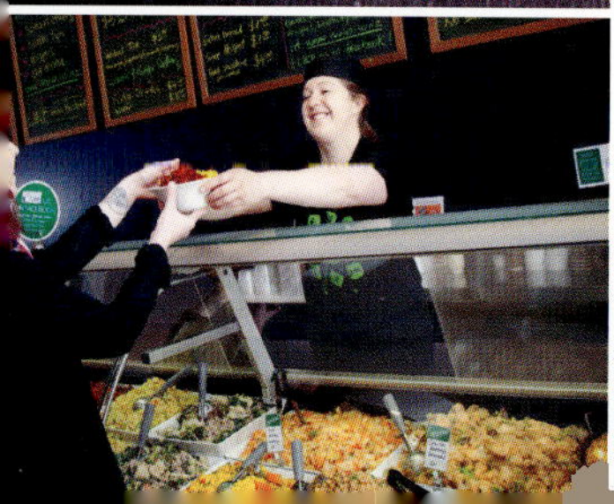
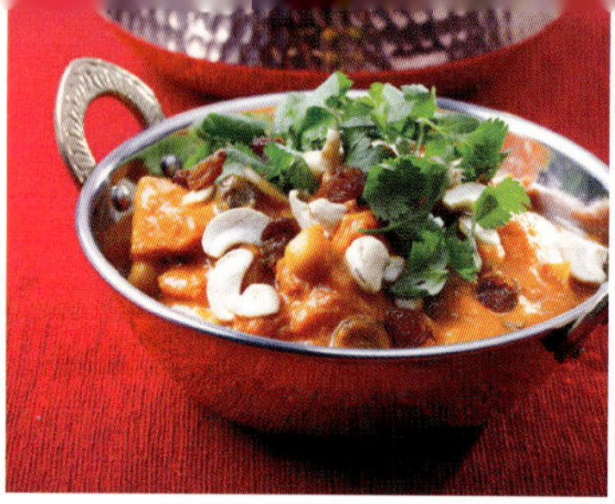
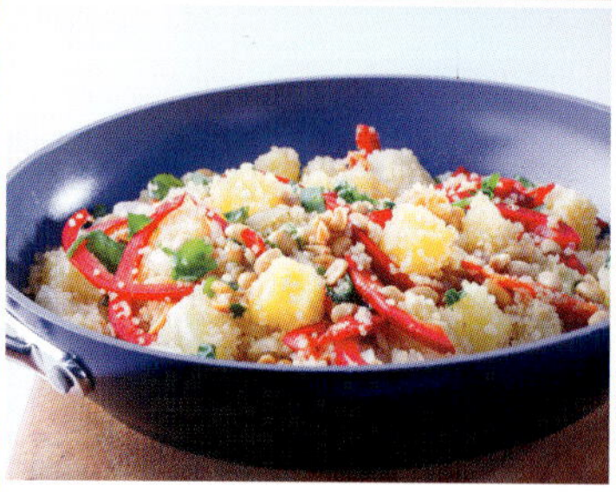
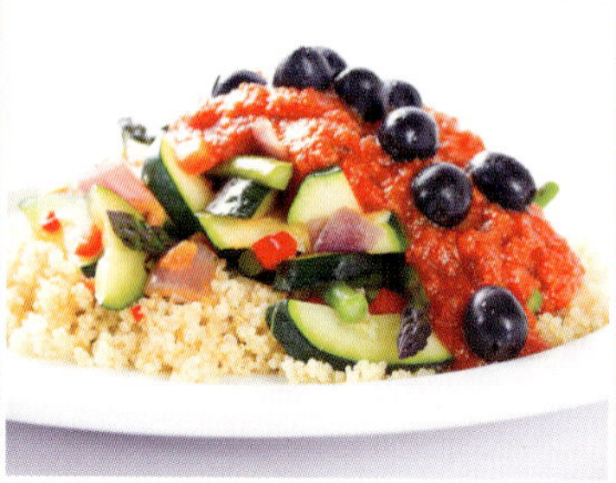
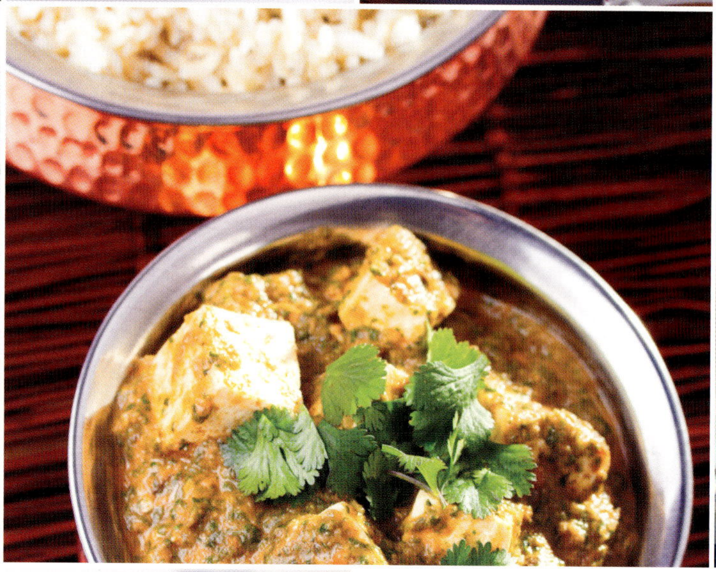
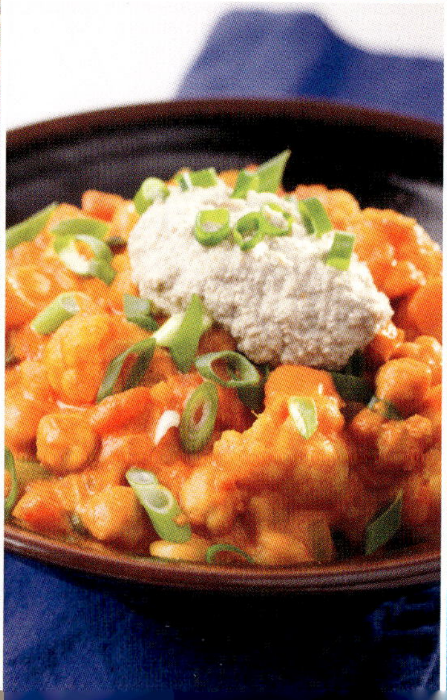
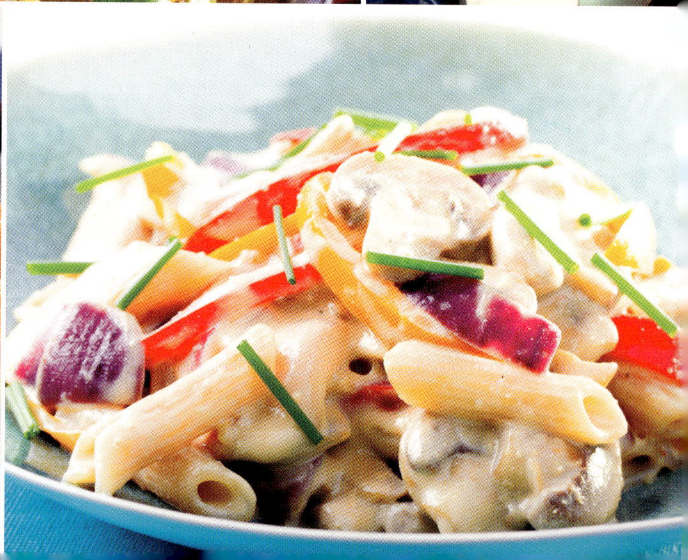
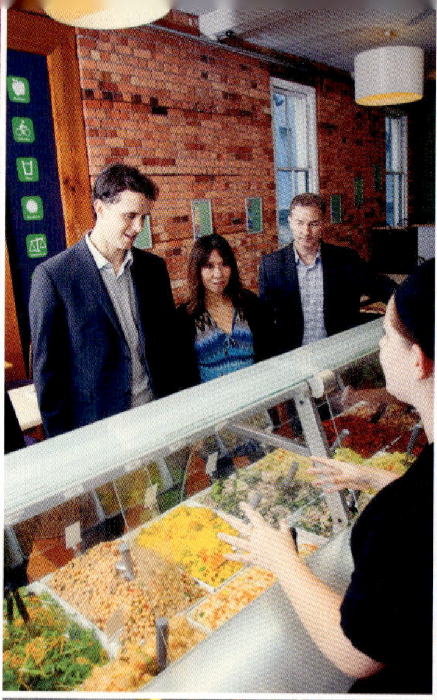
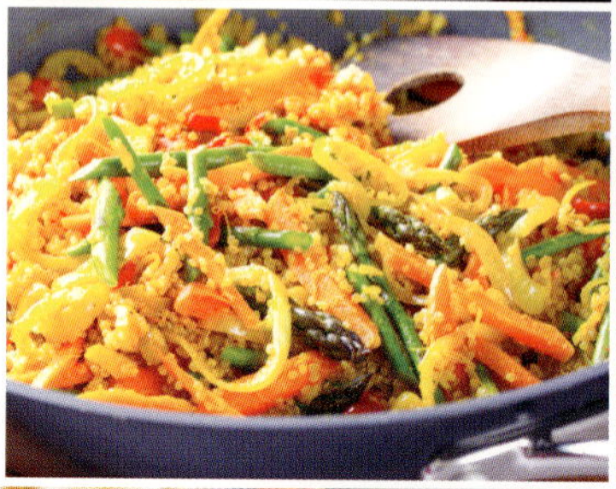
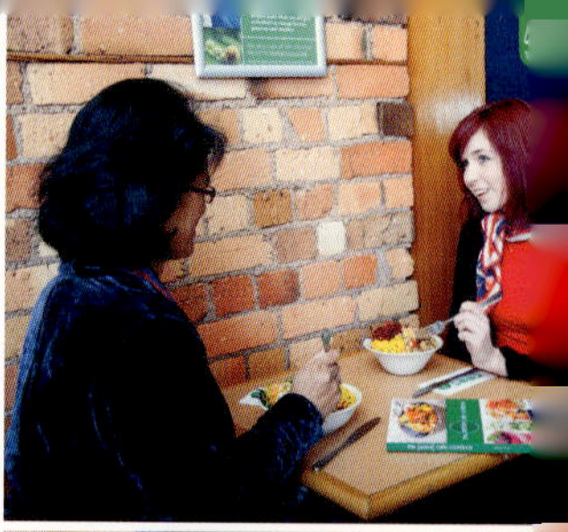
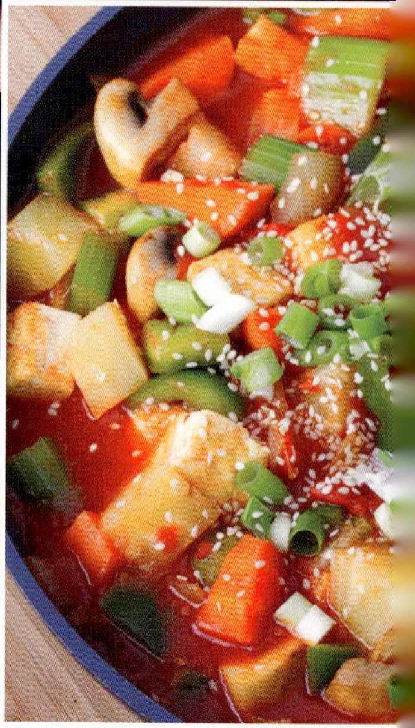
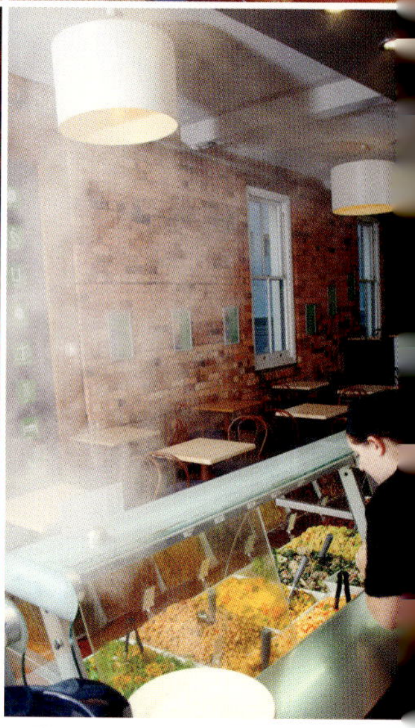

Hotpots & Stir Fries

Palak Paneer 54
Penne Alfredo 56
Thai Yellow Curry 58
Peanutty Pineapple Quinoa 60
Sweet & Sour Tofu. 62
Thai Massaman Lentil Casserole 64
Cauliflower & Chickpea Satay 66
Navratan Korma 68
Mediterranean Quinoa & Tomato Sauce 70
Italian Butter Bean Pasta. 72
Asparagus & Quinoa Stir Fry 74
Steam Fried Veges 76
Donburi. 78

Had no fennel seeds - seemed OK. Used fresh blettes in lieu of frozen spinach, & coconut milk instead of cream.

This is a dish inspired by Indian restaurants. They usually have a spinach mixture with lumps of cheese called paneer. This recipe uses tofu to replace this. Tofu is great as it soaks up strong flavours nicely. This dish is blended to create a creamy texture, however it is also a nice dish chunky so you can omit the blending stage for a different dish.

Palak Paneer

MAKES 6 X 1 CUP SERVES

- ½ cup urid dahl (split)
- 3 cups boiling water
- 1½ cups onion finely diced (around 1 onion)
- 2 teaspoons oil
- 1 tablespoon finely chopped ginger or ginger puree
- 2 cloves garlic finely chopped or crushed
- 1 tablespoon fennel seeds
- 1 packed cup frozen spinach (around 300g/10oz)
- 400g (12oz) can chopped tomatoes
- ½ cup coconut cream
- 1 teaspoon salt
- 300g (10oz) firm tofu cut into cubes
- garnish: coriander (cilantro)

1. In a pot cook the lentils and water for around 30 minutes or until soft. Drain off any water if there is any remaining. This will yield around 1½ cups.
2. In a pot saute the onion, oil, ginger, garlic and fennel seeds for around 5 minutes or until onion is soft.
3. Defrost spinach in a bowl of boiling water. Squeeze out any excess water.
4. Add spinach, tomatoes and lentils to onion mix. Keep heating and stirring until it starts bubbling.
5. Blend the mixture with a stick blender or put in a food processor or blender.
6. Add the coconut cream, salt and tofu.
7. Serve with coriander as a garnish.

I prefer the split urid dahl as it is faster to cook. If it is whole it will require more cooking time (and water) or you can soak overnight.

Fennel Seeds

These are bursting with an aniseed-like flavour and add an extra zest to curries. Make sure you cook them so they release their flavour. Some people do not like the taste so use sparingly - but I think it is great.

HOTPOTS & STIR FRIES 55

Penne Alfredo

Italian food tastes amazing however it is often accompanied by cheesy sauces and processed white flour. If you use a nut based sauce and some wholemeal pasta you can still make a great tasting meal but one that will be much better for your body!

MAKES 6 X 1 CUP SERVES

- 125g (4oz) wholemeal penne pasta (2 cups when cooked)
- 4 cups mushrooms thickly sliced (around 200g/6oz)
- 1 tablespoon oil
- 2 cloves garlic finely chopped or crushed
- 1 red capsicum (bell pepper) thinly sliced
- 1 yellow capsicum (bell pepper) thinly sliced
- 1 cup red onion diced into 1cm (½in) chunks (around 1 onion)
- chives for garnish

CREAMY SAUCE
MAKES 2 CUPS

- 1½ cups tofu (around 200g)
- 1 cup rice, soy or almond milk
- ½ teaspoon ginger puree
- 2 tablespoons nutritional yeast flakes
- 1 teaspoon salt
- 1 tablespoon honey
- garnish: chives

1. Cook pasta as per packet directions and drain.
2. Saute the mushroom and oil for a couple of minutes or until soft. Add garlic, capsicum and onion and saute for a couple more minutes until soft. All vegetables should be cooked through but still retain a little crunch.
3. Combine all sauce ingredients in a blender (or use a stick blender) and blend until smooth.
4. In a separate pot or small pan, heat the blended sauce mix for around 5 minutes or until well heated through and thick. Do not let it boil.
5. Combine all ingredients together and keep warm for a couple of minutes for the flavours to mingle.
6. Serve garnished with chives.

The sauce may seem too thin at first but it thickens up with cooking.

You can replace the tofu with cashew nuts to make the sauce!

Wholemeal Penne Pasta

This pasta is quite exciting to eat as the sauce goes into the middle of the pasta and seems to ooze out when eating. Make sure you find a good wholemeal version as most are made from processed white flour.

HOTPOTS & STIR FRIES 57

Thai Yellow Curry

I love Thai curries - they have so much flavour. Make sure you try all the different versions available which include red, green, yellow, Penang and Massaman.

MAKES 6 X 1 CUP SERVES

300g (10oz) pack firm tofu diced 1cm (½ inch)

1 tablespoon oil

1½ cups onion diced 1cm (around 1 onion)

1 tablespoon finely chopped ginger or ginger puree

1 cup red onion diced 1cm (around 1 onion)

1 courgette (zucchini) diced 1cm (½ in)

2 cups button mushrooms cut in half (around 150g/5oz)

1 red capsicum (bell pepper) diced 2cm (1 inch)

1 teaspoon turmeric powder

1 teaspoon Thai yellow curry paste

1½ cups hot water

2 cups broccoli florets (around 1 small head)

2 tablespoons honey or date puree

200ml (6oz) coconut cream

1 tablespoon lemongrass finely chopped

1 teaspoon salt

1. In a large pot saute the tofu and oil for 5 minutes or until the tofu starts to turn brown. Stir carefully so you do not break up the tofu.

2. Add the onion and ginger and saute for another 5 minutes or until the onion is soft.

3. Add the red onion, courgette, mushrooms and capsicum and saute for a further 5 minutes or until the mushrooms are starting to soften.

4. Add the turmeric and stir briefly.

5. Mix the curry paste with the water in a large cup and pour in.

6. Add the broccoli. Heat until it is bubbling.

7. Add remaining ingredients and heat through.

8. Serve with brown rice.

You can adjust the amount of curry paste to increase or decrease the hotness to your tastes.

Thai Yellow Curry Paste

Another fragrant Thai curry paste. Goes well with potatoes and green vegetables. I usually add some turmeric with this variant to increase the yellow colour. When using curry pastes mix them with a little water so they distribute evenly through the dish.

HOTPOTS & STIR FRIES 59

Here is another great stir fry combination. This dish can be served warm as a main meal, or served chilled as a salad.

Peanutty Pineapple Quinoa

MAKES 5 X 1 CUP SERVES

- ½ cup quinoa
- 1 cup boiling water
- 1½ cups onion finely diced (around 1 onion)
- 2 cloves garlic finely chopped or crushed
- 1 tablespoon ginger puree
- 1 tablespoon oil
- 1 teaspoon salt
- 450g (14oz) can pineapple chunks drained
- ½ red capsicum (bell pepper) thinly sliced
- ½ cup roasted peanuts
- ¼ cup fresh coriander (cilantro) chopped

1. Combine water and quinoa in a pot and simmer for around 12 minutes (lid on) or until cooked. ½ cup quinoa will yield around 1 cup cooked.
2. In a pan, saute the onion, garlic, ginger and oil for around 5 minutes or until soft.
3. Add the remaining ingredients and cook for a couple of minutes until everything is hot but still crunchy.
4. Serve with coriander for garnish.

Cook more quinoa than you need and keep in the fridge to use for breakfast or another meal.

While canned pineapple is convenient, if you can get whole pineapple it will improve the freshness and flavour.

Canned Pineapple

This is a great thing to have in your cupboard when pineapple is out of season or you do not have any on hand. Make sure you get the "natural juice" variety rather than in "syrup". Add to stir fries and it's great with anything sweet.

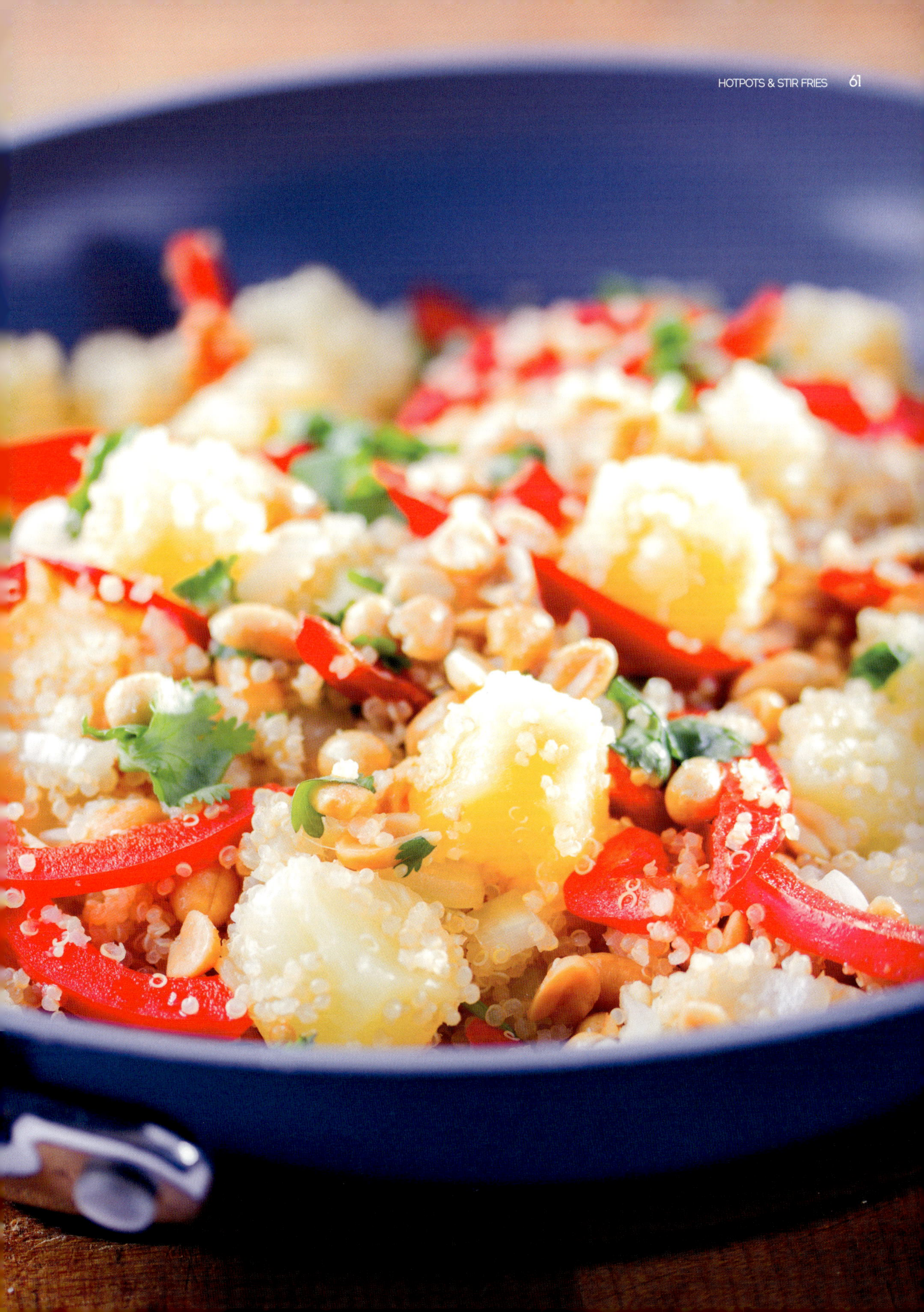

Sweet & Sour Tofu

MAKES 7 X 1 CUP SERVES

1½ cups onion diced into large cubes (around 1 large onion)

1 cup celery sliced (around 2 stalks)

1 green capsicum (bell pepper) cubed

2 cups carrots cut into half moons (around 1 large carrot)

2 tablespoons ginger puree or chopped ginger

2 cups (100g/3oz) mushrooms quartered

1 tablespoon oil

300g (10oz) tofu cut into large cubes

1 teaspoon salt

2 tablespoons honey or date puree

400g (12oz) can tomatoes chopped

400g (12oz) can cubed pineapple (reserve juice)

1 tablespoon cornflour or arrowroot

garnish: spring onions (scallions)

garnish: white sesame seeds

1. In a hot frying pan or wok saute the onion, celery, capsicum, carrots, ginger and mushrooms in the oil until just soft. Do not overcook – keep everything slightly crunchy.

2. In another frying pan saute the tofu in a little oil for around 10 minutes until golden. Add to the main pan or wok.

3. Add the salt, honey, tomatoes and pineapple (reserve the juice) and heat until just bubbling.

4. Mix the cornflour with the pineapple juice and stir through to thicken the sauce.

5. Garnish with spring onions and sesame seeds and serve on rice or rice noodles.

Golden Tofu

Tofu is a great protein source. You can add to curries raw, however it is nice when you pan fry or oven bake it first. Just add a little oil to a non-stick frying pan and gently saute the tofu for around 10-15 minutes until golden brown. Or bake mixed in a little oil for around 20 minutes at 150°C (300°F). Season with a little salt and add this to your dish.

HOTPOTS & STIR FRIES 63

Thai Massaman Lentil Casserole

MAKES 6 X 1 CUP SERVES

- 1 cup brown (crimson) lentils
- 1 cup dried figs diced
- 6 cups boiling water
- 1½ cups onion finely diced (around 1 large onion)
- 1 cup red onion largely diced (around 1 onion)
- 1 red capsicum (bell pepper) finely diced
- 3 cloves garlic finely chopped or crushed
- 1 tablespoon ginger puree or finely chopped ginger
- ½ tablespoon oil
- ½ teaspoon turmeric
- ¾ teaspoon salt
- ½ cup peanut butter
- 1 teaspoon Massaman Thai curry paste
- 1 cup water (for paste)
- 1 tablespoon honey
- 2 cups frozen peas
- garnish: ¼ cup coriander (cilantro)
- garnish: chopped peanuts

Massaman is thought to be a Persian based Thai curry flavour. It has many different spellings so any Thai curry paste that begins with the letter "M" will usually be the right one!

1. In a pot cook the lentils, figs and water for around 30 minutes or until soft. Drain.
2. Saute onions, capsicum, garlic and ginger in the oil for around 5 minutes or until soft.
3. Add turmeric and stir for around 30 seconds.
4. In a separate cup mix the salt, peanut butter, curry paste and water. Pour into the pan.
5. Add the lentils and remaining ingredients (except garnishes). Heat through so peas are not frozen.
6. Serve with peanuts and coriander to garnish.

This dish is great served with potatoes, rice and a fresh salad.

If you do not have Massaman curry paste any other variant will be fine.

Dried Figs

Tasty, soft, chewy, sweet, delicious! An instant flavour hit in any sweet dish and any salad or hot dish. Slice in strips or dice into small pieces. They are also a great snack eaten whole. Just cut off the stalks.

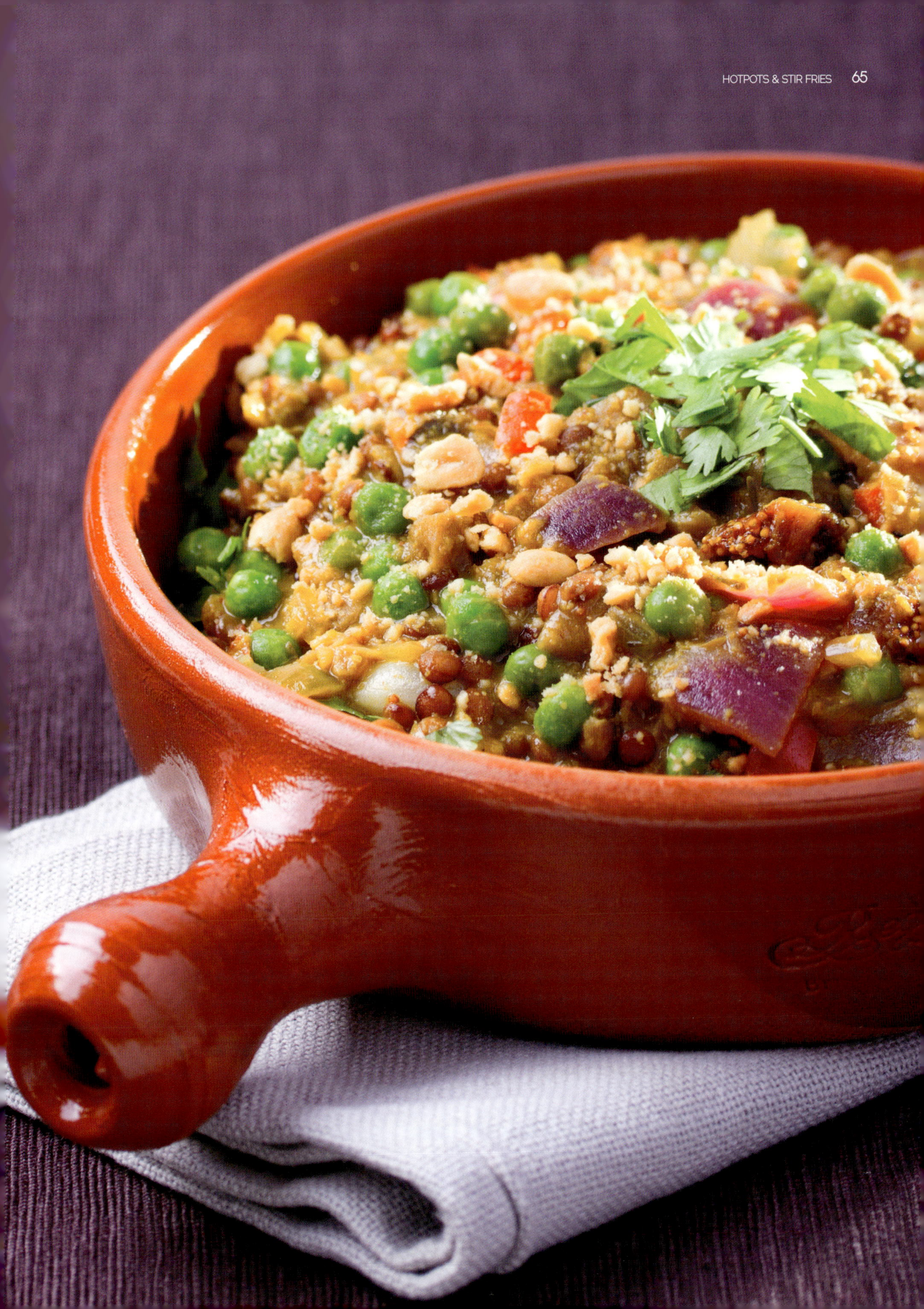

This is a great hearty winter-warming hotpot. Tomatoes, peanuts and ginger go together very well. Annelise, who was a recipe tester for me, received this recipe and was initially not happy as she has hated cauliflower since she was made to eat it as a child. But after she tested the recipe she loved it and it has revived her interest in this wonderful vegetable.

Cauliflower & Chickpea Satay

MAKES 10 X 1 CUP SERVES

1½ cups onions finely diced (around 1 onion)

2 cloves garlic finely chopped or crushed

1 tablespoon ginger puree or finely chopped ginger

1 tablespoon oil

2 teaspoons curry powder

1 teaspoon turmeric powder

1 teaspoon salt

2 tablespoons honey

2 x 400g (12oz) cans diced tomatoes

4 cups cauliflower (cut into small florets)

2 teaspoons arrowroot or cornflour mixed with ¼ cup cold water

1 cup red onion roughly diced (around 1 onion)

400g (12oz) can chickpeas (garbanzo beans)

200ml (6oz) coconut cream

4 tablespoons peanut butter mixed with ½ cup water

garnish: 1 cup sliced spring onions (scallions)

garnish: sunflower cream or hummus

1. In a pan saute the onion, garlic, ginger and oil for around 5 minutes or until soft.
2. Mix in the curry powder and turmeric for around 30 seconds to heat briefly.
3. Add the salt, honey and tomatoes and heat until it is just bubbling.
4. In a separate pot cook the cauliflower in boiling water for around 5 minutes or until just soft. Add to the main dish.
5. Mix the arrowroot and water and pour in.
6. Add red onion and chickpeas and heat until just about bubbling and the mixture thickens.
7. Stir in remaining ingredients and serve. Garnish with spring onions.

Serve with sunflower cream (The Revive Cafe Cookbook 1) or hummus (page 124).

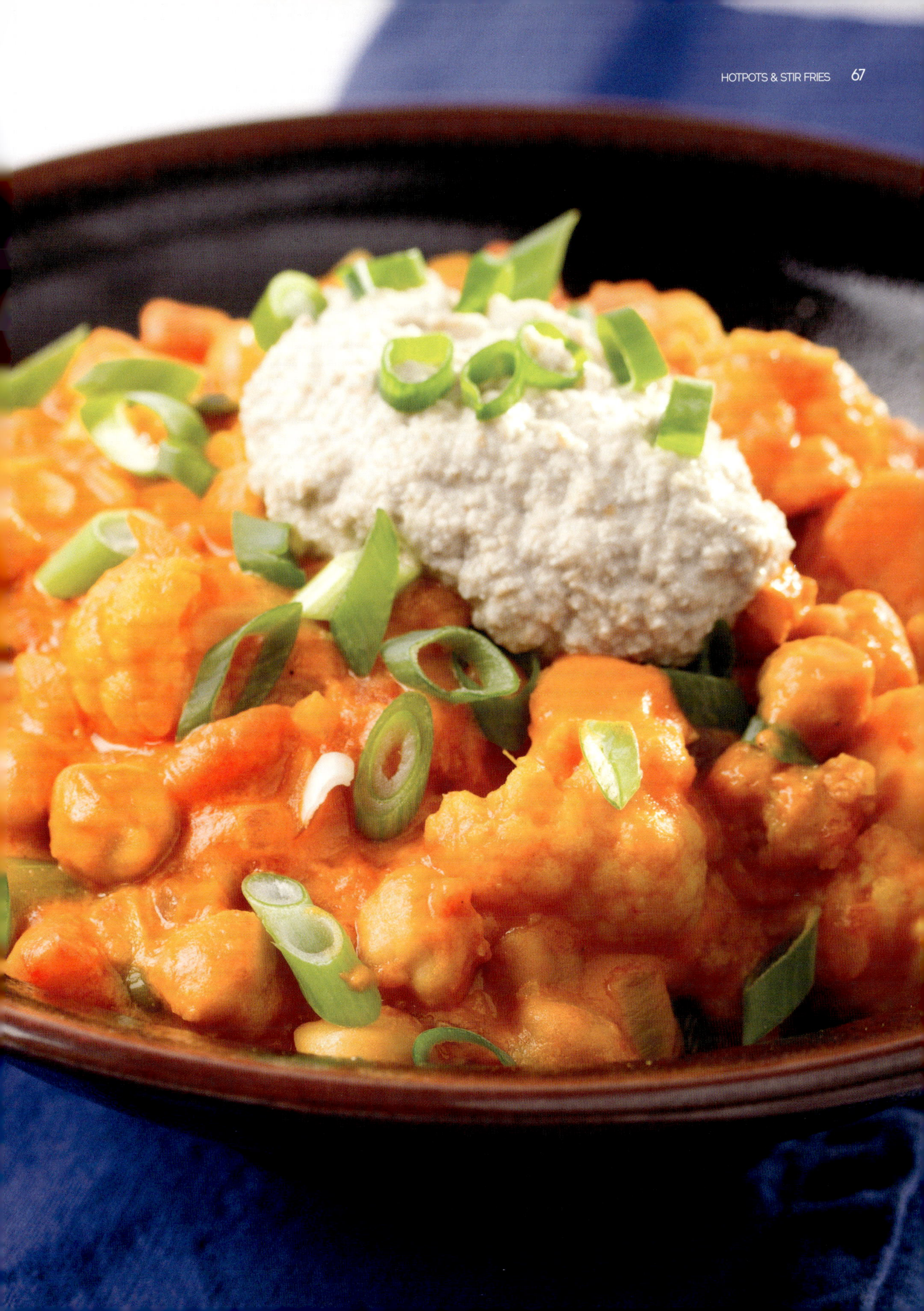

Navratan Korma

The crunchy nuts in this dish add great texture, while the spices create amazing fragrant flavours. The sultanas make it lovely and sweet too!

MAKES 6 X 1 CUP SERVES

1½ cups onion finely diced (around 1 onion)

2 cloves garlic finely chopped or crushed

1 tablespoon ginger finely chopped or ginger puree

1 tablespoon oil

½ teaspoon nutmeg

½ teaspoon clove powder

2 teaspoons cumin

1 teaspoon turmeric

1 teaspoon coriander

2 x 400g (12oz) cans chopped tomatoes

1 tablespoon honey or date puree

1 teaspoon salt

½ cup cashew nuts for puree

1 cup water

½ cup cashew nuts whole for the curry

1 cup sultanas

3 cups pumpkin well roasted cut into cubes

garnish: coriander (cilantro)

1. In a pot saute the onions, garlic, ginger and oil for around 5 minutes or until clear.
2. Add the spices and mix for around 30 seconds to heat.
3. Stir in the tomatoes, honey and salt and heat until it is nearly bubbling.
4. In a blender (or using a stick blender) blend the cashew nuts and the water into a thick cream and add to the curry.
5. Add the cashew nuts, sultanas and pumpkin.
6. Garnish with fresh coriander and some additional sultanas and cashews.
7. Serve with freshly cooked brown rice.

You can use roasted kumara (sweet potato) or potato instead of pumpkin.

If you want a lower fat option this will also taste good without the cashew cream.

Soaking Dried Fruit

Dried fruit like sultanas, raisins, dates, figs and apricots are great in many meals. Over time they lose their moisture which makes them dry and hard. It is easy to make them plump again. Simply soak in boiling water for around 5 minutes to re-hydrate. Drain before serving. You can use cold water however it will take hours rather than minutes.

HOTPOTS & STIR FRIES 69

This is not a recipe as such but more of a serving suggestion with some vegetables and a great tomato sauce.

Mediterranean Quinoa & Tomato Sauce

SERVES 4

2 cups boiling water

1 cup quinoa

1 cup red onion diced (around 1 onion)

2 cups courgettes (zucchini) halved and sliced (around 2 large courgettes)

12 stalks asparagus

1 red capsicum (bell pepper) diced

1 tablespoon oil

½ teaspoon salt

2 cups Italian tomato sauce (page 134)

garnish: ½ cup black olives

1. In a pot simmer the water and quinoa (lid on) for around 12 minutes or until cooked. This will yield around 2 cups cooked.

2. In a pan saute the onion, courgette, asparagus, capsicum and oil for around 5 minutes or until soft. Do not overcook.

3. Sprinkle over salt and stir in.

4. Make the Italian tomato sauce or reheat if you have already made it.

5. Serve vegetables over the quinoa and lavishly pour over the tomato sauce. Garnish with olives.

Asparagus

A nice fresh spring vegetable. Needs to be only lightly cooked or steamed so it retains its crunch. To prepare simply bend the stalks and they will automatically snap off at the end where it starts to get woody and stringy.

HOTPOTS & STIR FRIES 71

This is a good fast dinner in minutes. It is good if you already have some Italian tomato sauce made in your fridge or freezer. It is amazing how some meals can be prepared so simply with some ingredients already in your refrigerator.

Italian Butter Bean Pasta

MAKES 4 X 1 CUP SERVES

2 cups Italian tomato sauce (page 134)

1 cup red onion roughly diced (around 1 onion)

1 cup courgettes (zucchini) sliced (around 2 courgettes)

1 red capsicum (bell pepper) sliced

2 teaspoons oil

400g (12oz) can butter beans

wholemeal or gluten free pasta of your choice

1. Make the tomato sauce.
2. In a pan saute the onion, courgette, capsicum and oil for around 5 minutes or until just starting to go soft.
3. Add the tomato sauce and butter beans to the vegetable mix.
4. Serve over pasta.

You can also use a store-bought tomato sauce if you do not have time. However once you see how easy it is to make your own tomato sauce and how amazing it tastes you will never buy pre-made tomato sauce again.

Italian Tomato Sauce

Make your own tomato sauce using the recipe on page 134. Make a large batch and store in the fridge or freezer. You can use with pasta, pizzas, cannelloni, lasagne and in many other meals.

HOTPOTS & STIR FRIES 73

Asparagus & Quinoa Stir Fry

This stir fry uses vegetables that are long and pointy. It is a very simple recipe. Try to cut them a similar size and length for a great texture when eating.

MAKES 6 X 1 CUP SERVES

- 2 cups boiling water
- 1 cup quinoa
- 1½ cups onion sliced (around 1 onion)
- 2 cloves garlic finely chopped or crushed
- 1 tablespoon finely chopped ginger or ginger puree
- 2 cups carrot cut into matchsticks (around 2 medium carrots)
- 1 tablespoon oil
- ½ teaspoon turmeric
- 12 stalks asparagus diagonally sliced
- 1 red capsicum (bell pepper) cut into small cubes
- ½ teaspoon salt
- 2 tablespoons honey or date puree

1. In a pot simmer the water and quinoa (lid on) for around 12 minutes or until cooked. This will yield around 2 cups cooked.
2. In a large pan saute the onion, garlic, ginger, carrots and oil for around 5 minutes or until the onion has gone clear.
3. Add the turmeric and mix well for around 30 seconds.
4. Add the asparagus and capsicum and fry for another 3-5 minutes or until the vegetables have softened.
5. Add the cooked quinoa, salt and honey and mix well.

To prepare the asparagus bend all the pieces together with your hands to snap them. They will snap automatically at the end of the soft part before the woody ends that you do not want.

If asparagus is out of season you can use frozen green beans instead.

HOTPOTS & STIR FRIES   75

Sometimes it is nice to have simple vegetables - here is a great recipe for a colourful and fresh side dish.

Steam Fried Veges

MAKES 5 x 1 CUP SERVES

2 cups green beans (tops chopped off)

1 red capsicum (bell pepper) sliced

1 orange capsicum (bell pepper) sliced

1 red onion sliced

2 cups courgette (zucchini) sliced (around 1 large courgette)

2 cups carrot cut into matchsticks (around 1 large carrot)

1 tablespoon oil

optional: 2 tablespoons finely chopped ginger or ginger puree

optional: 2 cloves garlic finely chopped or crushed

½ teaspoon salt

2 tablespoons honey

1 tablespoon black sesame seeds

1 tablespoon white sesame seeds

1. Prepare vegetables into long strips.
2. Pour oil in a hot non-stick pan, add vegetables and mix together.
3. Optional: add ginger and/or garlic if you want some extra flavour.
4. Put the lid on and saute/steam for around 5 minutes - shaking every minute. The vegetables will sweeten with the frying and also cook by steaming with the lid on.
5. Add the salt, honey and sesame seeds.

Cook the vegetables so they are still crunchy.

You can cut the vegetables in advance and keep in an airtight container ready to put in the pan when required.

Matchsticks

This is a good way to cut coloured vegetables for great visual appeal. You need a sharp knife. The trick is to cut the vegetable into slices first, and then slice them into thin sticks (or matchsticks). You can also get attachments for food processors that can do this automatically!

HOTPOTS & STIR FRIES 77

This is a Japanese dish. Donburi means "bowl". Here is a healthy version you can make at home. It is great when you have friends around as you can put all of the ingredients in the center of the table and everyone can customise their own dish.

Donburi

SERVES 4

300g (10oz) firm tofu

1 tablespoon oil

2 tablespoons honey

3 tablespoons soy sauce or tamari for tofu

2 cups brown rice cooked

2 tablespoons soy sauce or tamari for the bowl

2 tablespoons runny honey

BOWL INGREDIENTS

½ cup bamboo shoots

½ red capsicum (bell pepper) sliced

1 cup carrot cut into matchsticks (around 1 medium carrot)

½ avocado diced

1 stalk Asian greens of your choice sliced

garnish: ½ teaspoon black sesame seeds

garnish: ½ teaspoon white sesame seeds

1. Slice the tofu into slabs 1cm (½in) thick.
2. Put the oil in a hot pan and gently fry the tofu on each side until it forms a crispy skin. This will take up to 10 minutes. Add the honey and soy sauce to the pan and mix briefly. Set aside.
3. In each of your serving bowls put a ½ cup of cooked rice. Drizzle with soy sauce and honey.
4. Add the "bowl" ingredients on top to your taste.
5. Place the tofu on top and sprinkle with sesame seeds.

If you are serving as a group arrange all the ingredients in individual bowls on the table and let everyone make their own bowl.

Use any seasonal vegetables for this dish.

HOTPOTS & STIR FRIES 79

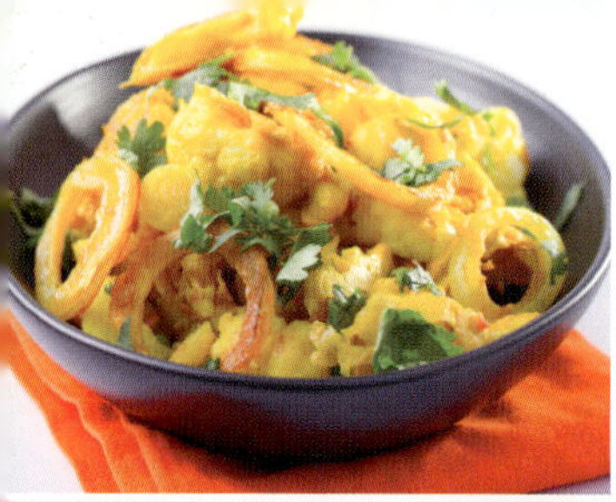
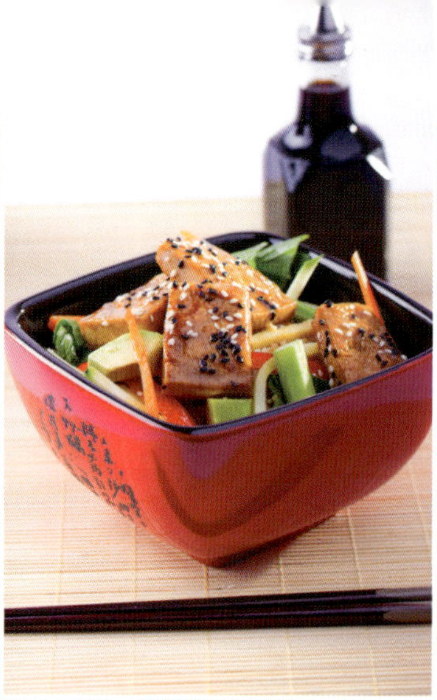
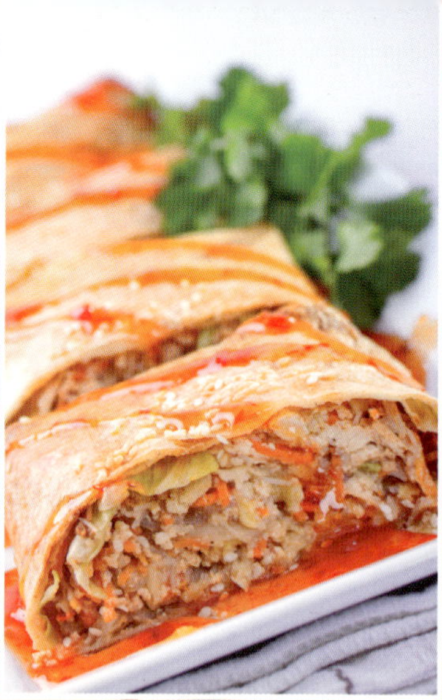
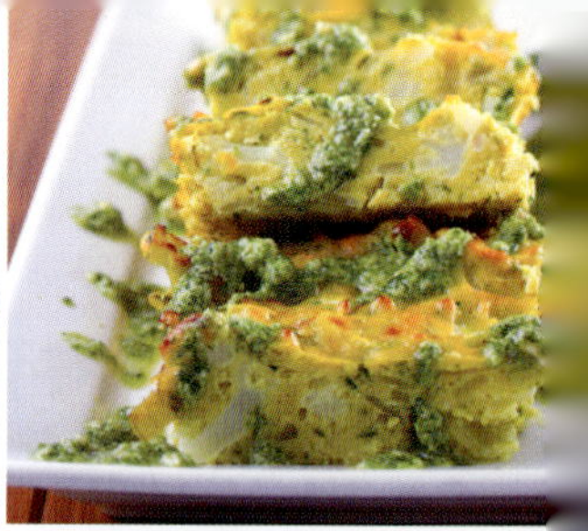
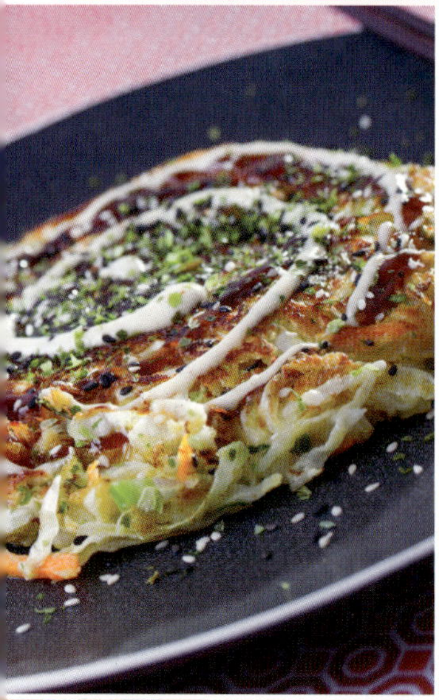
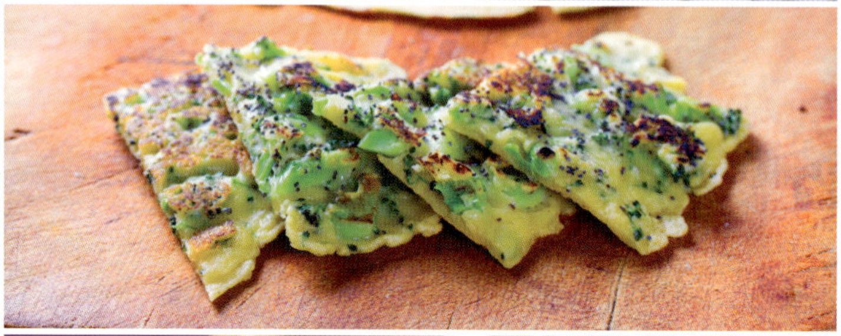
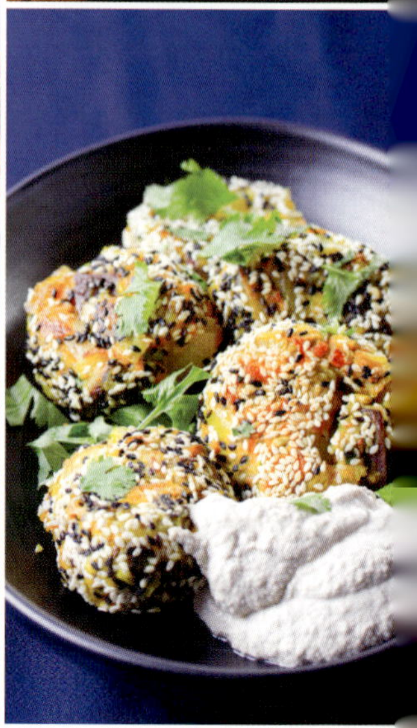
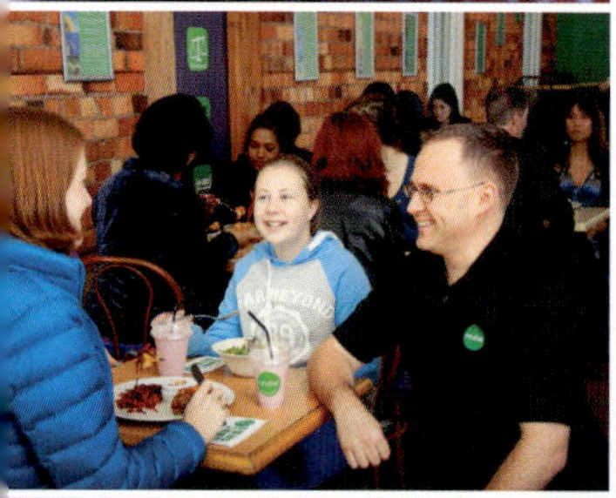
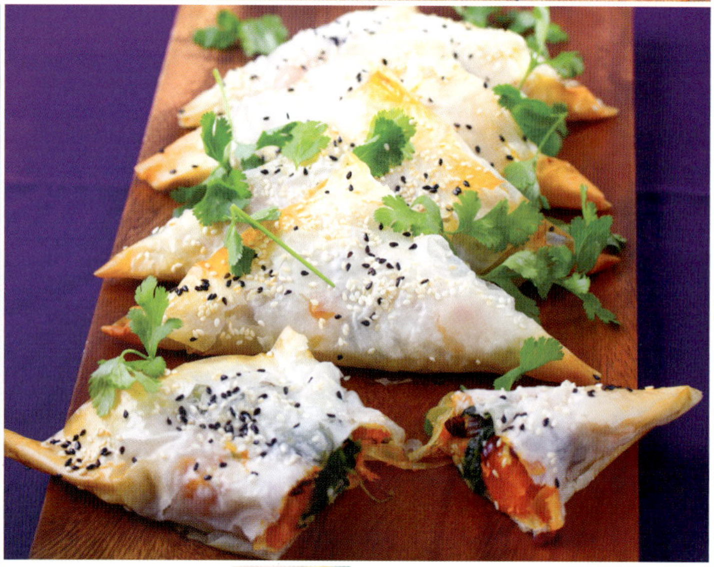
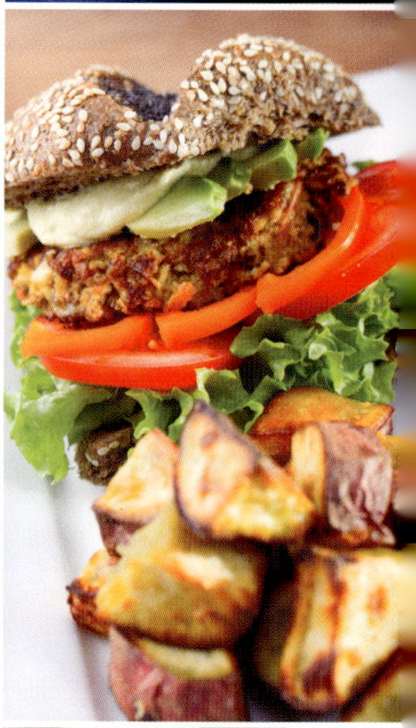
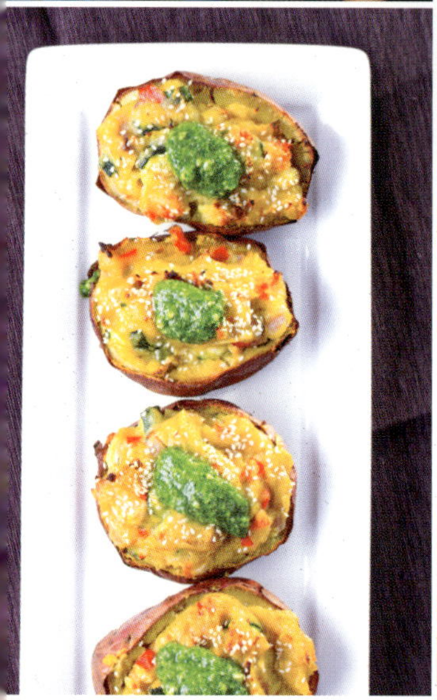
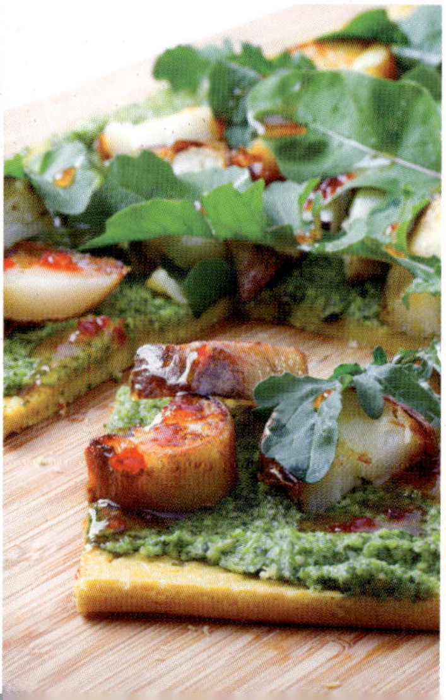
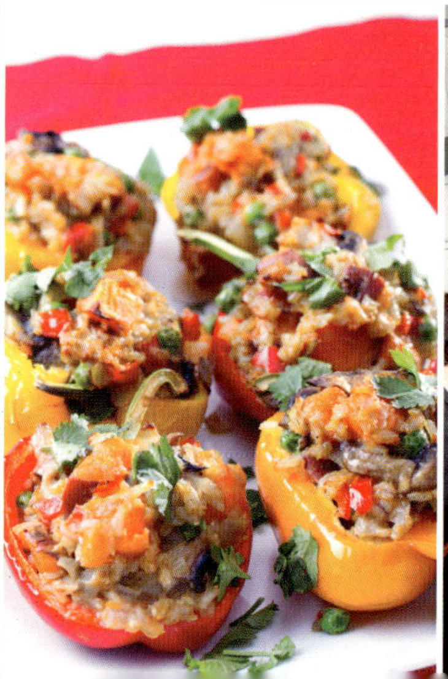
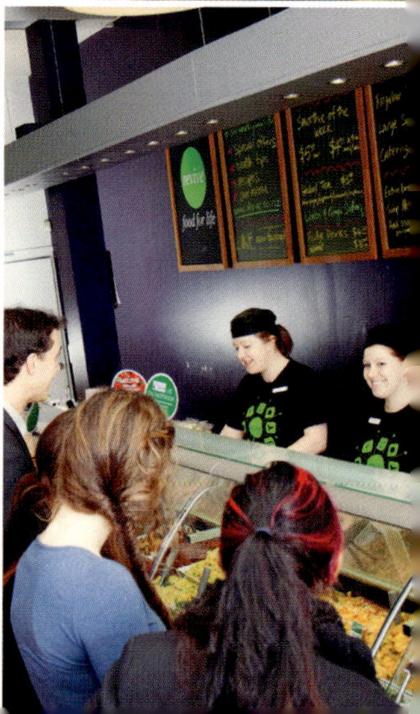
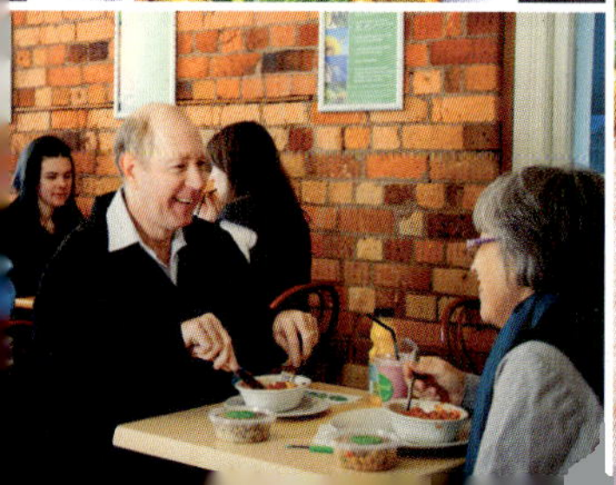

Main Meals

Scrummy Stuffed Sweet Potato 82

Kumara & Carrot Cakes 84

Pumpkin & Cranberry Filo Parcels 86

Okonomiyaki (Japanese Pancake) 88

Vegetable Pakoras 90

Broccoli Infused Flatbread 92

Summer Burger 94

Smoked Stuffed Peppers 96

Pesto & Potato Chickbread Pizza 98

Courgette & Cauliflower Bake 100

Thai Spring Rolls 102

This dish is amazingly yummy. I was pleasantly surprised when I made it. The trick is to make sure you slow roast the kumara, do not rush the process. These are most satisfying to pick up and eat with your hands.

Scrummy Stuffed Sweet Potato

MAKES 6 SERVES

3 large kumara (sweet potato)

1 cup red onion finely diced (around 1 onion)

2 cloves of garlic finely chopped or crushed

¾ cup red capsicum finely diced (bell pepper)

1 cup finely diced courgette (zucchini) (around 1 courgette)

½ cup cashew nuts raw roughly chopped

1 tablespoon oil

½ cup soy or almond milk

½ teaspoon salt

optional: 1 tablespoon chilli finely diced

garnish: 1 tablespoon white sesame seeds

garnish: basil or coriander (cilantro) pesto

1. Brush or spray the kumara with a little oil and bake for 1 hour at 150°C (300°F) or until soft.

2. Carefully slice in half. Scoop out the centres into a mixing bowl leaving a thin layer of flesh inside to give it some strength.

3. In a pan saute the onion, garlic, capsicum, courgette, cashews and oil for around 4 minutes or until just starting to soften. You still want them to retain their shape.

4. Combine the kumara flesh with the onion mixture and stir in the milk and salt. Add some chilli if you are brave enough.

5. Fill the kumara with the mixture and heap it up. Sprinkle the sesame seeds on top.

6. Bake for around 10 minutes at 150°C (300°F).

7. Optional: garnish with basil or coriander pesto.

If your kumara are different shaped sizes that is fine - you will have a more interesting looking meal!

MAIN MEALS 83

These are great for meals, picnics or make small versions as finger food. The kumara is a great binding ingredient.

Kumara & Carrot Cakes

MAKES 18 CAKES

4 cups orange kumara diced (sweet potato)

1 tablespoon oil (for kumara)

1½ cups onion diced (around 1 onion)

1 cup grated carrot (around 1 medium carrot)

1 tablespoon oil

½ cup sunflower seeds

1 teaspoon ground coriander

1 teaspoon ground cumin

1 teaspoon turmeric

1 teaspoon salt

½ cup chickpea (besan/chana) flour

1 cup fresh coriander (cilantro) roughly chopped

½ cup water

¼ cup black sesame seeds

¼ cup white sesame seeds

oil for shallow frying

garnish: coriander (cilantro)

garnish: sunflower cream or hummus

1. Roast the kumara and oil for around 15 minutes at 180°C (350°F) or until very soft. Mash roughly so you can still see the cubes.

2. In a pan saute the onion, carrot, oil and sunflower seeds for around 5 minutes or until the onion is soft.

3. Add the spices and mix for around 30 seconds.

4. In a bowl combine the mashed kumara, onion mix, salt, chickpea flour, fresh coriander and water and mix into a dry mash. You may need to add a little more water to make them just moist.

5. Heat a non-stick pan with a little oil.

6. Scoop out ¼ cup measures and press together with your hands and form into balls.

7. Put the sesame seeds in a bowl, and dip the balls into them and roll around.

8. Shallow fry in a little oil for around 3 minutes per side.

9. Serve with a garnish of fresh coriander and a dollop of sunflower cream (The Revive Cafe Cookbook 1) or hummus (page 124).

Modify this recipe with your favourite vegetables and spices!

MAIN MEALS 85

At the church I attend we put on a Mother's Day lunch each year to make the Mums feel special. For some reason I am always asked to do the catering. This year I planned to do these and make it a little special. I started making squares, parcels, rectangles, rolls, baskets and other shapes. It wasn't working and we were minutes away from the time we needed to get them in the oven so we could have lunch ready. Then my Russian friend Andrey tried some triangles and made them look awesome! And they then became a Revive recipe.

Pumpkin & Cranberry Filo Parcels

MAKES 8 PARCELS

2 cups pumpkin or butternut diced

1 teaspoon oil (for pumpkin)

1½ cups onion diced (around 1 onion)

1 teaspoon oil (for onion)

½ cup dried cranberries

½ teaspoon salt

1 cup frozen spinach defrosted (around 300g/9oz)

8 sheets filo pastry - size around 30x20cm (12x8in)

oil for brushing

garnish: 1 teaspoon black sesame seeds

garnish: 1 teaspoon white sesame seeds

garnish: fresh coriander (cilantro)

1. Mix the diced pumpkin with 1 teaspoon of oil on a baking tray. Bake for around 20 minutes at 180°C (350°F) or until soft.

2. In a pan saute the onion and 1 teaspoon oil for around 5 minutes or until soft.

3. In a mixing bowl combine pumpkin with onion, cranberries, salt and spinach.

4. Put 2 sheets of filo pastry onto your chopping board and cut in half lengthwise so you have 2 long pieces on top of each other.

5. Spoon ½ cup of the mix onto the bottom right corner. Fold into a triangle. Keep folding over into triangles until you have used all the pastry. There will be around 4-5 folds required depending on the size.

6. Using a brush, oil the filo parcels lightly. You can also use an oil spray. Make sure the tips and sides are covered as these burn the easiest.

7. Garnish with a sprinkle of sesame seeds.

8. Bake in the oven at 150°C (300°F) for around 15 minutes or until crunchy.

9. Garnish with fresh coriander.

Do not overmix as it is nice to have some clumps of the different ingredients.

I have never found wholemeal filo pastry, only filo made from white flour. However as it is very light it only makes up a fraction of the weight of the dish, a small amount of white flour is not worth worrying about.

MAIN MEALS 87

Handwritten notes:
- Very nice
- ½ quantity good for 2 people
- Used red currant chilli jelly instead of plum sauce: ok
- Didn't have seaweed flakes.

Okonomiyaki (Japanese Pancake)

Our friend Heather who loves experimenting with new dishes encouraged me to try this meal. This is a Japanese dish often referred to as the Japanese Pizza. It normally contains white flour and meat, so this is my healthier version. It is very flexible so use any ingredient combinations you like.

MAKES 2 PANCAKES

BATTER
- 1 cup chickpea (besan) flour *(½ cup)*
- ¾ cup water *(3/8 cup)*
- ½ teaspoon salt *(¼ tsp)*
- ½ tablespoon ginger *(¼ Tbsp)*

6 CUPS THINLY SLICED VEGETABLES: *(3 cups)*
- cabbage
- red onion
- carrot
- spring onions (scallions)
- mushroom finely diced

GARNISHES
- sesame seeds black
- sesame seeds white
- aioli (page 134) or tofu mayo (page 132)
- plum sauce or other red sauce
- seaweed flakes

1. Mix the batter ingredients together.
2. Slice the vegetables thinly or use a food processor with a slicer blade.
3. In a separate bowl, mix ½ cup of the batter with 3 cups of the vegetable mix. It will seem like there is not enough batter however it will go further than you think!
4. Heat a non-stick frying pan with a little oil.
5. Put the mix in the pan and flatten down. It will need to be flattened a few times as the cabbage reduces in size.
6. Cook 1-2 minutes each side or until golden.
7. Serve with swirls of sauce, aioli and sprinkles of sesame seeds and seaweed flakes.

You can use a second heated frying pan to flip the pancake into. If you do not have one you can put a plate on top and turn upside down and then slide the pancake back into the pan.

Seaweed flakes are usually available from Japanese grocery stores or you could use finely chopped parsley for a similar effect.

MAIN MEALS

This little Indian side dish is usually deep fried. However these pakoras still work very well shallow frying and are delicious. You can also use other vegetables like broccoli, eggplant, carrots and roasted kumara. As they are not being deep fried, most vegetables will need to be lightly pre-cooked.

Vegetable Pakoras

SERVES 4

1 cup chickpea (chana/besan) flour

½ teaspoon ground coriander

1 teaspoon salt

½ teaspoon ground turmeric

½ teaspoon garam masala

2 cloves garlic crushed

1 cup water

oil for frying

3 cups (around ¼ head) cauliflower florets sliced

1 large onion sliced into rings

garnish: fresh coriander (cilantro)

1. Sift all dry ingredients into a bowl. Add garlic and water and mix well into a smooth batter.

2. Slice cauliflower and onion. Rather than preparing round florets, cut through the cauliflower so you have slices about 1cm (½ inch) thick.

3. Cook or steam the cauliflower for around 5 minutes to soften it.

4. Place vegetables individually into the batter and totally cover with the mixture. You can use your fingers or tongs.

5. Heat a non-stick frying pan and put in a splash of oil for each batch.

6. Fry each side for around 2 minutes or until golden brown.

7. Garnish and serve immediately.

These are also great served as finger food with some dips!

You may need to add more water or flour to the batter depending on the consistency.

Shallow frying

This is a great way to cook many things in a pan rather than deep frying. However if you use a good non-stick frying pan you will find that you need very little oil. Some people shallow fry with cups of oil which is basically deep frying. Do not do this!

MAIN MEALS 91

It is very easy to create a flatbread with any vegetables of your choice. It is almost like a supercharged pancake.

Broccoli Infused Flatbread

MAKES 2

½ cup fine chickpea (besan/chana) flour

½ cup water

½ teaspoon salt

1 teaspoon oil

¾ cup raw broccoli finely chopped (around 2 florets)

1 teaspoon poppy seeds

a little oil for frying

1. In a mixing bowl, mix the flour and half the water until smooth, then add the rest of the water, salt, oil and mix until combined.
2. Finally mix in the broccoli.
3. Heat a small non-stick frying pan with a little oil.
4. Pour in half of the mixture (for the first flatbread) and swirl around so the pan is evenly coated. Cook the first side for around 1 minute.
5. Sprinkle some poppy seeds and a little more oil (or use a spray). Flip and cook the other side for around a minute or until cooked but not burnt.
6. Cut into wedges and serve immediately.

Making Chickpea Flour

If you do not have any available, you can simply put some raw chickpeas into a coffee grinder and blend until very fine. Coffee grinders are excellent for making flours from grains, nuts and pulses in small quantities. The trick is to only do small amounts at a time so you can get it nice and fine.

MAIN MEALS 93

Summer Burger

MAKES 5 BURGERS

1½ cups onion finely diced (around 1 large onion)

1 cup grated carrot (around 1 medium carrot)

2 cloves garlic finely chopped

1 teaspoon oil

1 teaspoon dried oregano

2 cups sliced mushrooms (around 100g (3oz))

3 tablespoons soy sauce or tamari

½ cup chickpea (besan/chana) flour

1 teaspoon salt

1 tablespoon nutritional yeast flakes

oil for frying

BURGER COMPONENTS

wholemeal burger buns

hummus

avocado

capsicum (bell pepper)

frilly lettuce

tomato

In my first year at Revive we had these delicious burgers on our menu. Unfortunately it turns out that combining ready to serve "cabinet" food with meals ordered from the kitchen does not work in our busy lunch environment. We had to take them off the menu. Here you can relive our first days with this tasty burger.

1. In a pan saute the onion, carrot, garlic and oil until soft.
2. Combine the onion mix with all the other ingredients in a bowl.
3. Form into ½ cup sized burger patties.
4. In a hot pan fry in a little oil. Cook for 5-10 minutes per side or until firm and golden brown.
5. Serve on wholemeal burger buns with fresh salad ingredients.

Serve with oven roasted kumara (sweet potato) chunks on the side.

Frilly Lettuce

This is the best lettuce for sandwiches and burgers as its texture gives height and interest and lots of crunch. Its official name is lollo bionda (the red version is called lollo rossa).

MAIN MEALS 95

These look and taste fantastic. In the early days of Revive we put these on the menu and quickly discovered that our customers did not buy them. They would walk past and say "they look lovely" but end up buying something familiar like a frittata or lasagne. I thought I would include them in this book anyway as they are awesome and quick to make.

Smoked Stuffed Peppers

MAKES 6

1 cup long grain brown rice

2 cups boiling water

3 cups orange kumara (sweet potato) diced (around 1 large kumara)

1 teaspoon oil (for kumara)

1½ cups onion finely diced (around 1 large onion)

2 cloves garlic finely chopped or crushed

2 teaspoons smoked paprika

4 cups sliced button mushrooms (around 200g (6oz))

1 teaspoon oil

1 cup frozen peas

½ teaspoon salt

1 cup soy or almond milk

3 capsicum (bell peppers) assorted colours

garnish: coriander (cilantro)

1. In a pot simmer the rice and boiling water for around 25 minutes (lid on) or until the water has disappeared.

2. Mix the kumara with oil and bake for 15 minutes at 150°C (300°F) or until soft.

3. In a pan saute the onion, garlic, smoked paprika, mushrooms and oil (with the lid on) until the mushrooms are soft.

4. In the pan add the cooked rice, kumara, peas, salt and milk and stir. Mash the kumara so it starts to break apart.

5. Cut the capsicum in half long ways and lightly oil or spray them.

6. Spoon the rice mix into the peppers and place on an oven tray. Lightly oil or spray the tops.

7. Bake for 15-30 minutes at 150°C (300°F) or until the capsicum is soft.

8. Serve with coriander as garnish.

If your peppers want to tilt over, just slice a flat strip off the bottom and they should stand straight.

If you want a more mushroom focus, include more and leave the kumara out.

MAIN MEALS 97

This is an awesome pizza variation using chickbread. The combination of pesto, potato, sweet chilli and rocket is just amazingly fresh and unique. See, you do not need dripping cheese and white flour to enjoy a pizza!

Pesto & Potato Chickbread Pizza

MAKES 12 SLICES TO SERVE 6 PEOPLE

4 cups potatoes cut into 2cm (1in) cubes (around 3 potatoes)

1 tablespoon oil

½ teaspoon salt

3 cups chickpea (besan/chana) flour

3 cups water

1 teaspoon onion powder

½ teaspoon garlic powder

2 tablespoons oil

1 teaspoon salt

oil for brushing the tray

1 cup basil pesto (page 135)

2 tablespoons sweet chilli sauce

1 cup fresh rocket or baby spinach leaves

1. Combine the potatoes, oil and salt on an oven tray and bake at 150°C (300°F) for around 40 minutes or until soft.

2. In a mixing bowl, combine the chickpea flour with 1 cup of the water and mix well. When mixed, slowly add the rest of the water while mixing. This process will help avoid clumps.

3. Add the onion powder, garlic powder, oil and salt and mix well.

4. Select an oven tray (with sides) around 30x40cm (12x16in). Brush well with oil.

5. Pour in the chickpea mix and bake at 180°C (350°F) for 15 minutes. The mixture may seem to be too runny however this is normal.

6. Spread the pesto on the base, sprinkle the potatoes on top and garnish with the rocket. Drizzle sweet chilli sauce all over.

Rocket (Rucola) Leaves

This salad green has an exquisite peppery flavour and is great to use where you would normally use another salad green. I usually plant some seedlings in my garden in spring - it grows well and I have more than enough to last throughout the summer.

MAIN MEALS 99

I found a similar dish to this in a vegetarian restaurant in Nepal. It tasted great, however it was dripping with cheese and eggs and not all that healthy. It was served on an amazing brass curved rectangular plate. I attempted to buy a plate from the restaurant so I could use for photography in this cookbook, however they would not part with it even when I offered what I thought was a significant sum. So here is my healthier version of this dish, with a normal white plate.

Courgette & Cauliflower Bake

MAKES 6 LARGE SLICES

- 1½ cups onions roughly chopped (around 1 large onion) [¾]
- 1 tablespoon oil
- 3 cloves garlic finely chopped or crushed
- 3 cups courgettes (zucchini) grated (around 3 medium) [1½]
- 3 cups small chopped cauliflower florets [1½]

CHICK MIX

- 1½ cups chickpea (besan/chana) flour [¾]
- 1½ cups soy or almond milk [¾]
- ¼ teaspoon turmeric [½]
- 1 cup cashew nuts [½]
- 1 teaspoon salt [½ tsp]
- 1 teaspoon baking powder [½ tsp]
- 1 tablespoon nutritional yeast flakes [½ Tbs]
- garnish: basil or coriander pesto

1. In a pot saute the onions, oil, garlic and courgettes for around 5 minutes or until soft.
2. Add the cauliflower to a pot of boiling water and cook for around 5 minutes or until just soft.
3. In a blender (or use a stick blender) add the chick mix ingredients and process until smooth.
4. In a mixing bowl combine all ingredients.
5. Spray or lightly oil a baking tray around 400 x 200mm (16 x 8in). Pour the mixture in.
6. Bake for 30 minutes at 180°C (350°F) or until cooked through.
7. Garnish with basil or coriander pesto (page 135).

Slice into 6 pieces for a main meal, or into 24 pieces for finger food.

---
if you want it to brown on top you can spray a little oil on top near the end of the cooking process.

Nutritional Yeast Flakes

This flaky substance adds a nice savoury flavour to dishes and some dressings. It is usually found in health or whole food stores.

MAIN MEALS 101

Nice stirfry = filling. Don't bother with burritos/tortillas

Thai Spring Rolls

At parties and Thai restaurants you can get these little deep fried Thai spring rolls. I decided to try a healthier, larger version that we could sell as a meal at Revive and here is the recipe! You can also add 1 teaspoon of your favourite Thai curry paste to the onion mixture for some Thai flavours (although this is not truly authentic).

MAKES 7

- 100g (3oz) thin rice noodles (vermicelli)
- 1 tablespoon finely chopped ginger or ginger puree
- 2 cloves garlic finely chopped or crushed
- 1 cup carrots cut into matchsticks (around 1 carrot)
- 1½ cups onions finely sliced (around 1 onion)
- 1 tablespoon oil
- 2 cups white (green) cabbage thinly sliced
- 300g (10oz) firm tofu crumbled
- ½ teaspoon salt
- 1 tablespoon honey or date puree
- 2 tablespoons soy sauce or tamari
- 2 tablespoons sweet chilli sauce
- ½ cup coriander (cilantro)
- 1 cup mung bean sprouts
- 6 large wholemeal burritos or tortillas
- oil for brushing
- 1 tablespoon sesame seeds
- garnish: coriander (cilantro)
- garnish: sweet chilli sauce

1. In a pot stand the rice noodles with boiling water until they are soft. Usually takes around 2-5 minutes, however you are best to check the instructions on your noodles. Drain and set aside.

2. In a different pan saute the ginger, garlic, carrots, onion and oil for around 5 minutes or until they start to soften.

3. Add the cabbage and tofu and cook for another 5 minutes or until cabbage is wilted.

4. Add the salt, honey, soy sauce, sweet chilli sauce and noodles and stir around until mixed and hot.

5. Add the coriander and sprouts and stir together.

6. Place 1 cup of the mixture in the middle of a burrito. Bring sides in first and then wrap. Place on a baking tray lined with paper. Repeat for all 6 wraps.

7. Brush with a little oil and sprinkle the sesame seeds on top for garnish.

8. Bake for 10 minutes at 180°F (350°F) or until crisp and heated through.

Note: the spring rolls in the photo are whole rolls cut in half.

Thin Rice Noodles

Often called vermicelli, these noodles are great for spring rolls and for serving hotpots. They generally go clear when cooked so have a nice effect on most meals. And they take minutes to cook with some boiling water, although you are best to follow the packet instructions.

MAIN MEALS 103

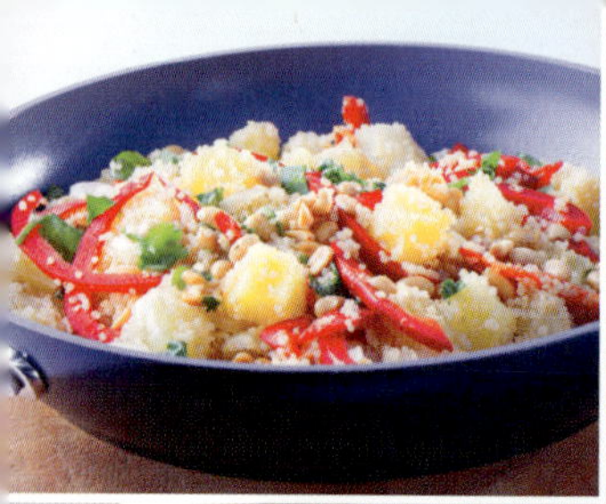
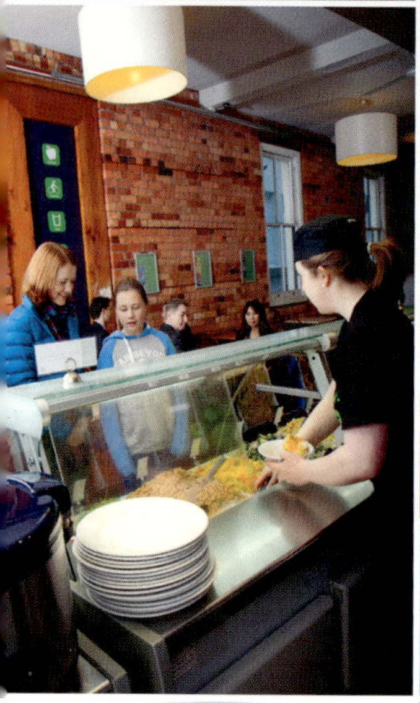
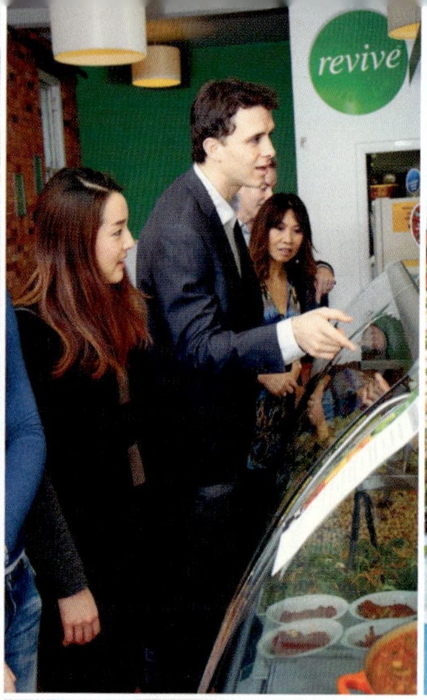
revive
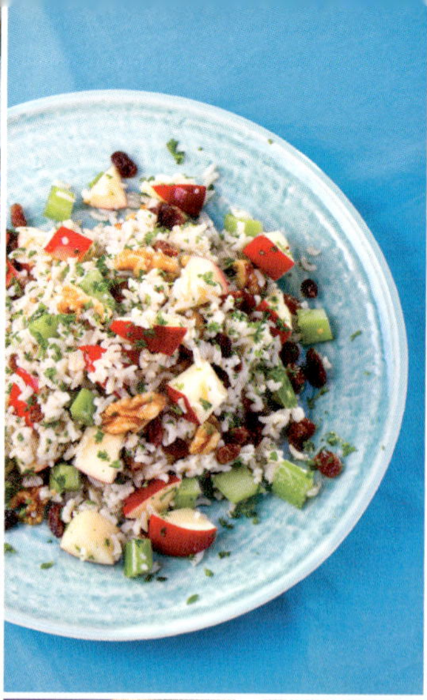
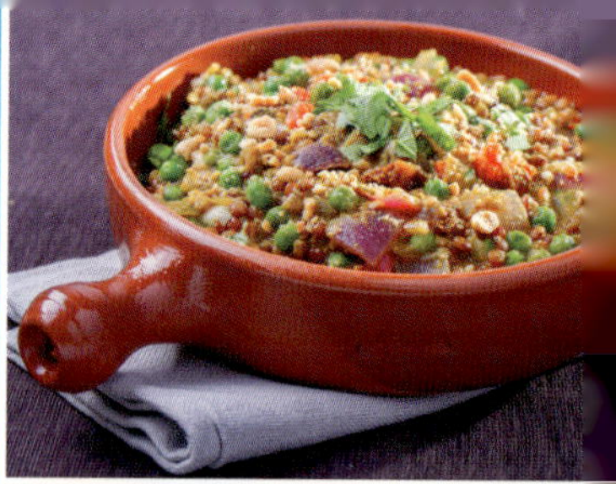
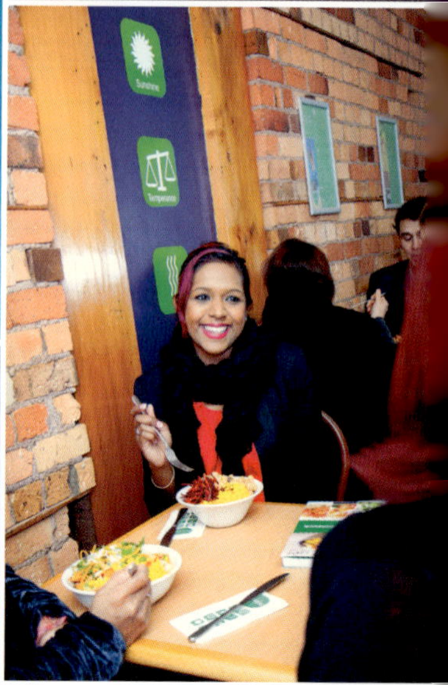
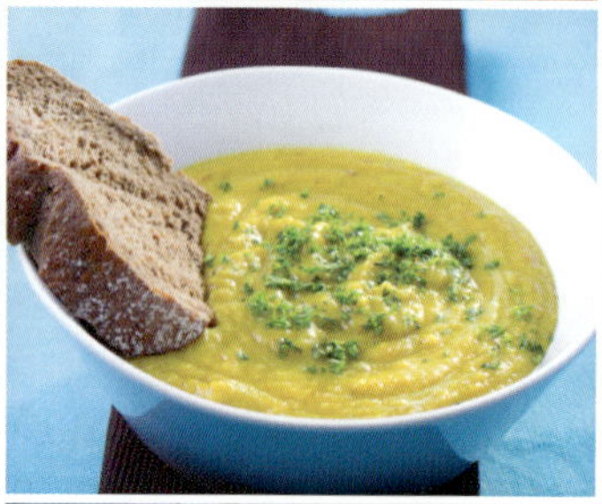
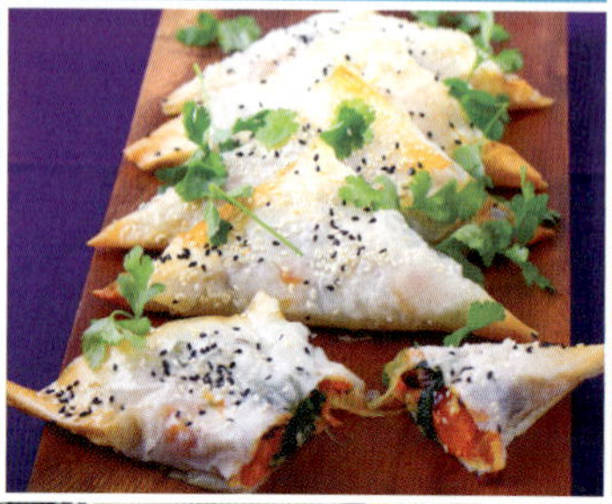
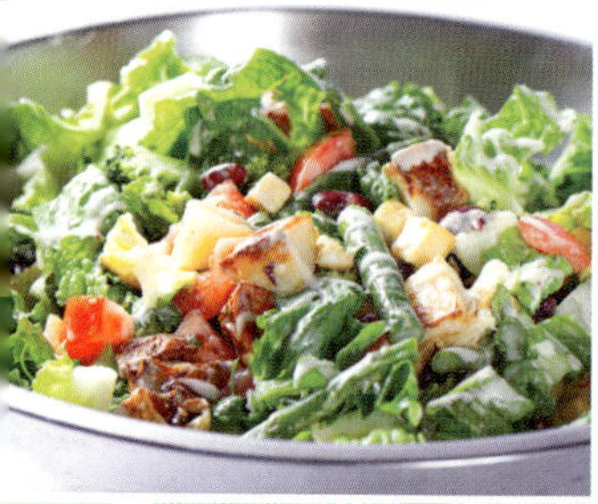
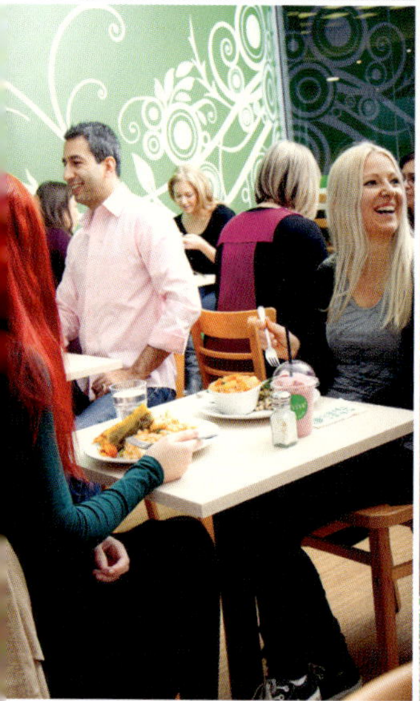
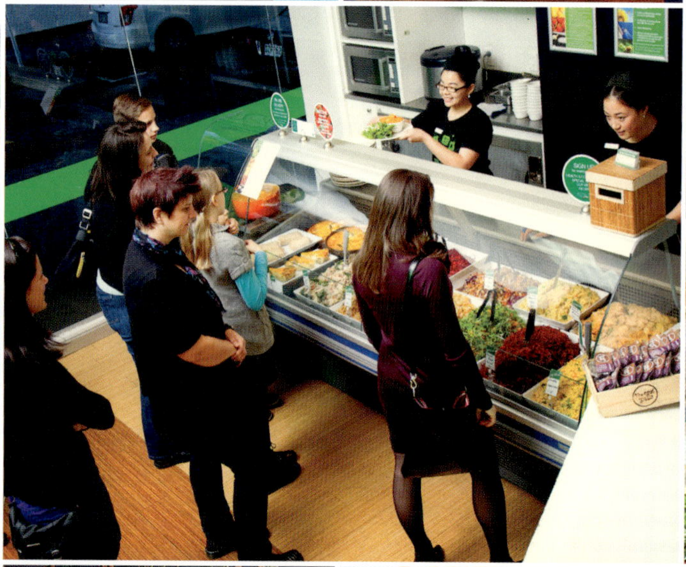
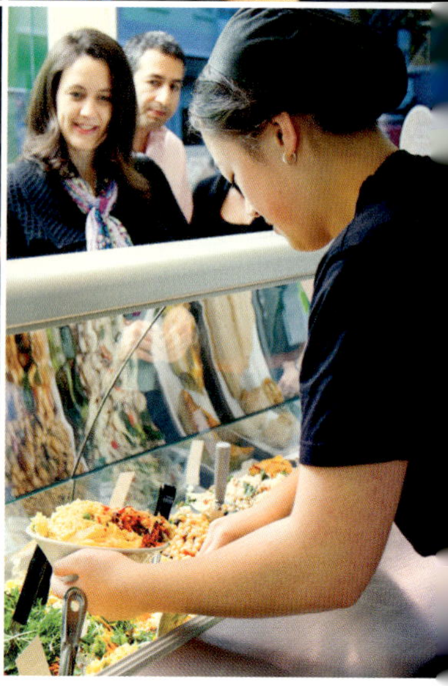
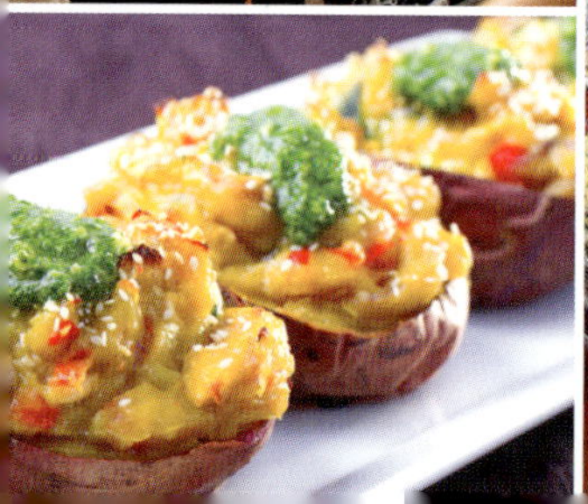
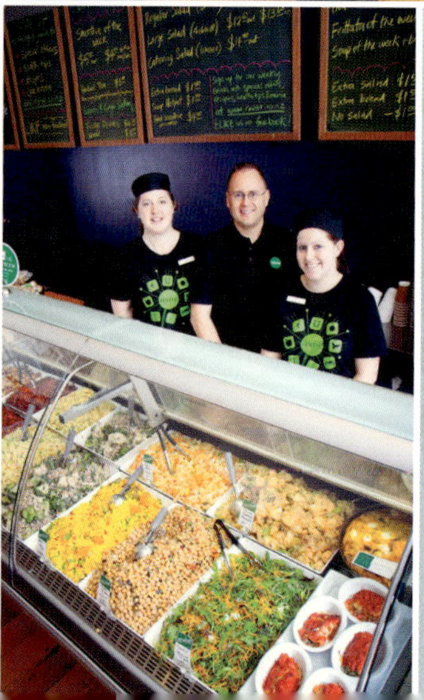
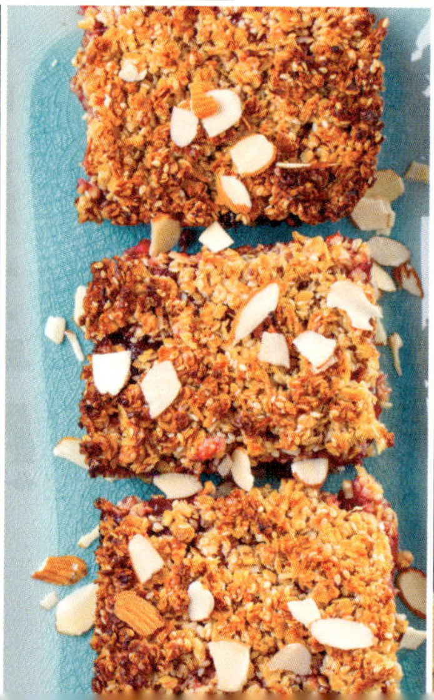
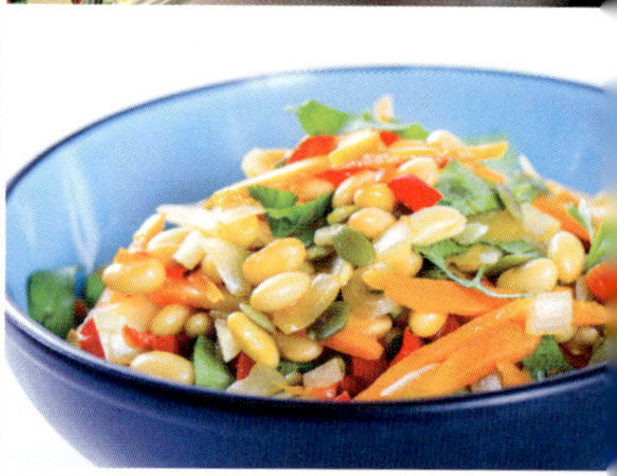
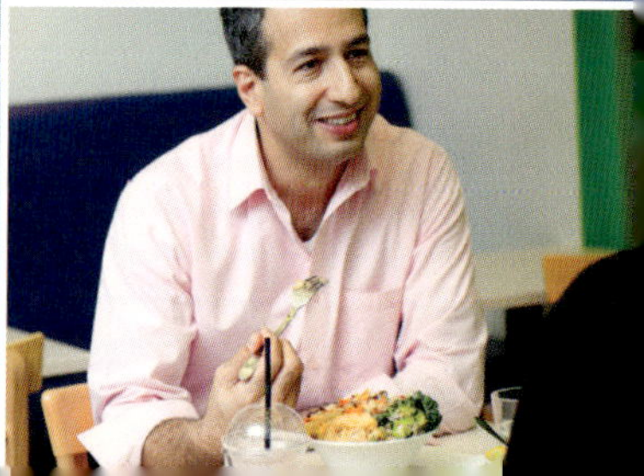

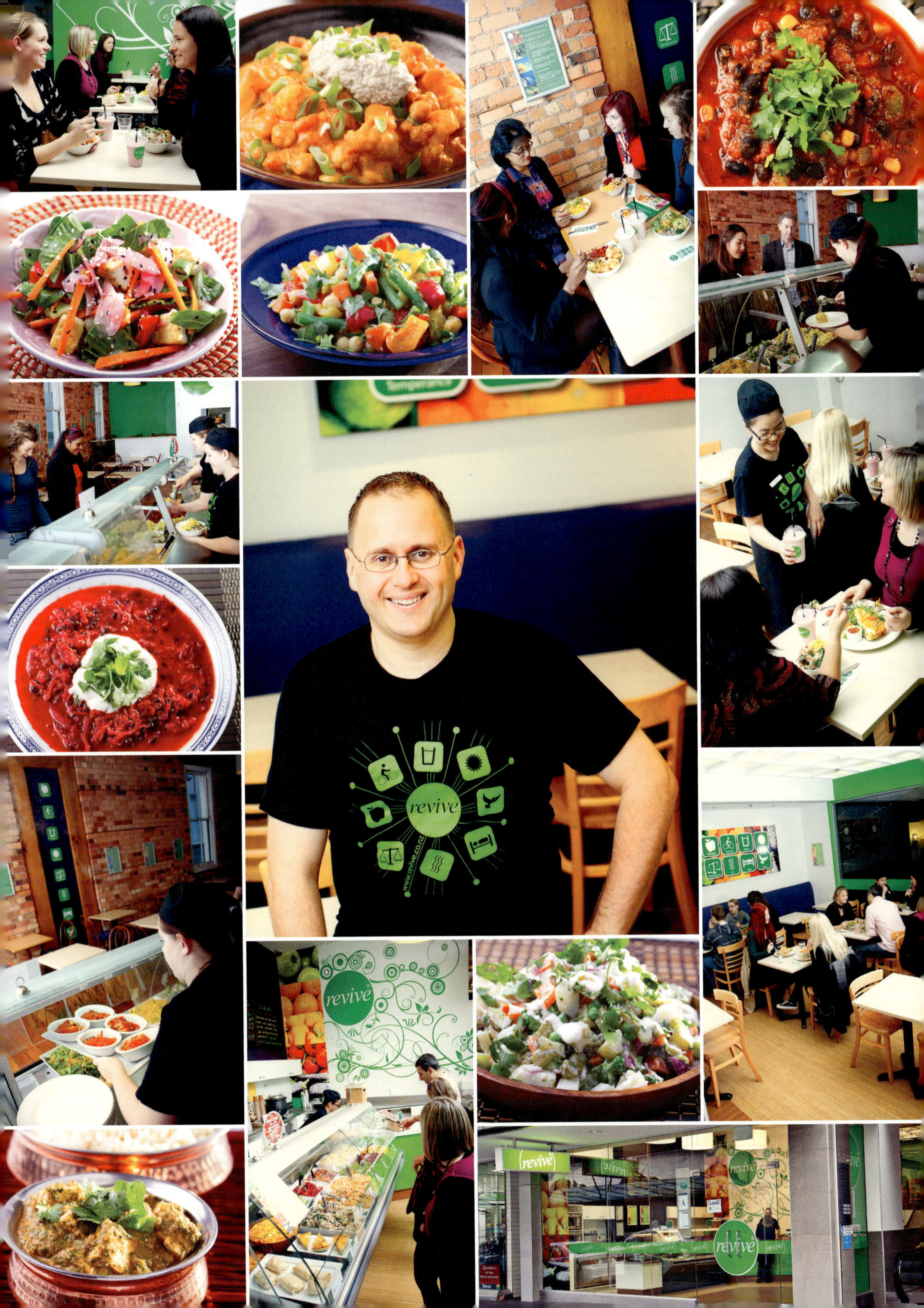
revive
www.revive.co.nz
revive
revive

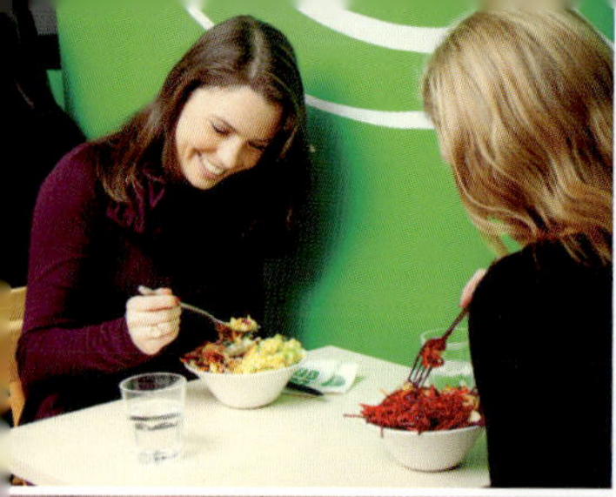
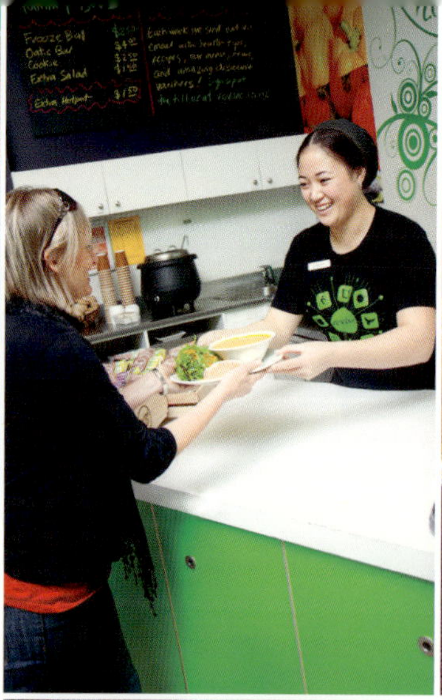
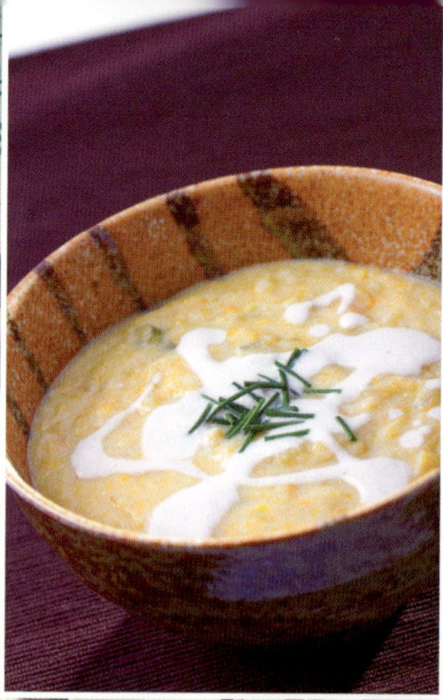
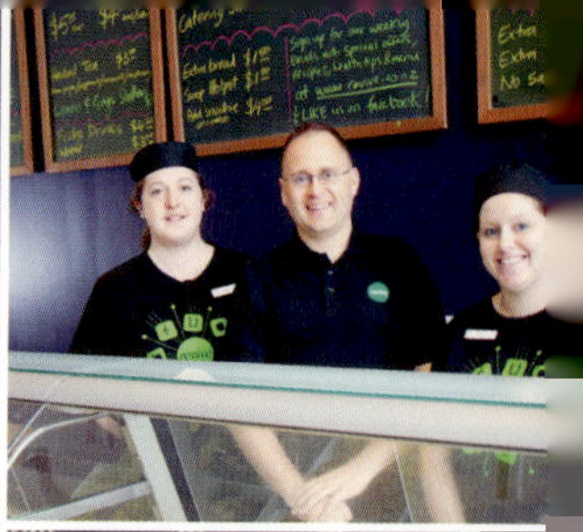
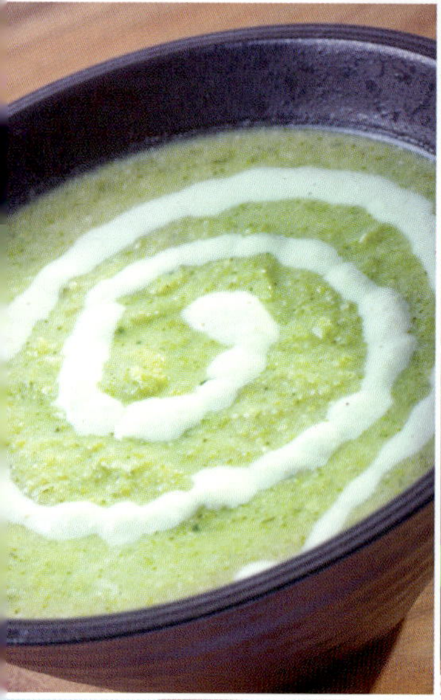
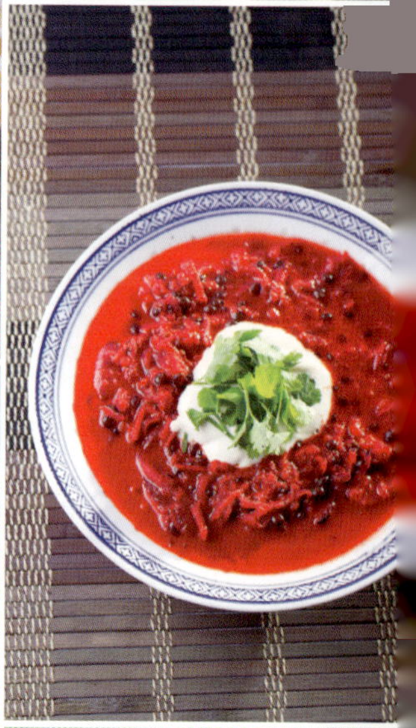
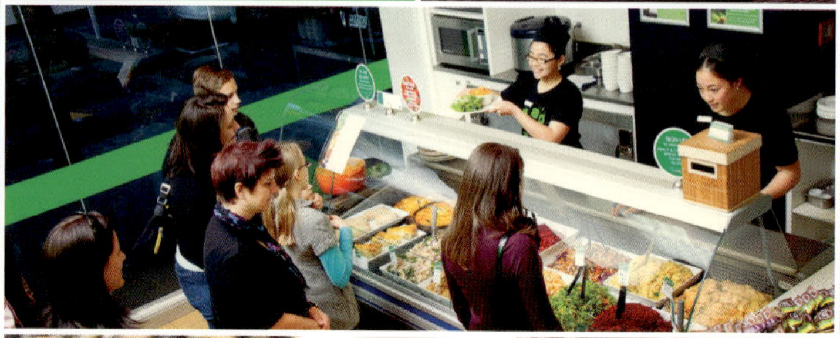
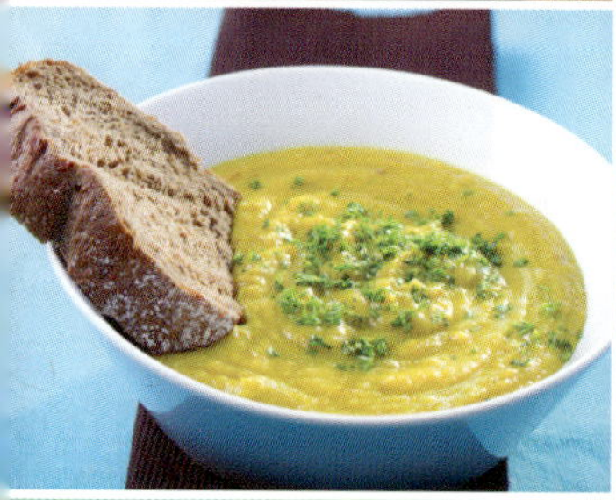
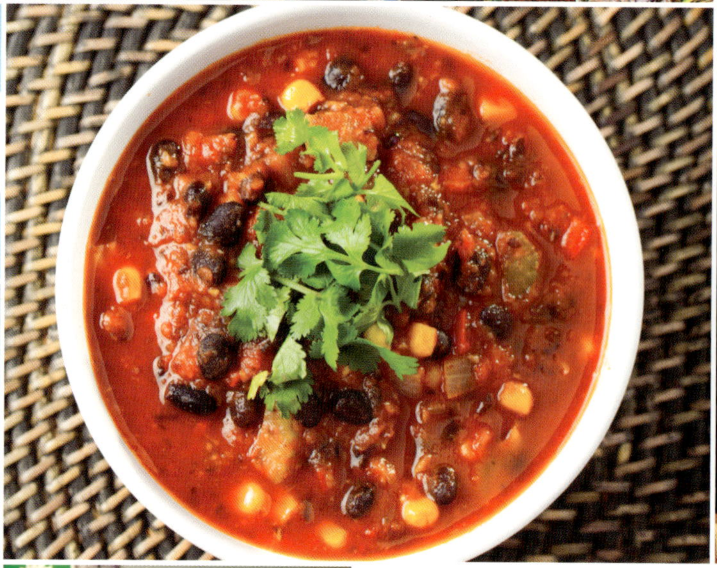
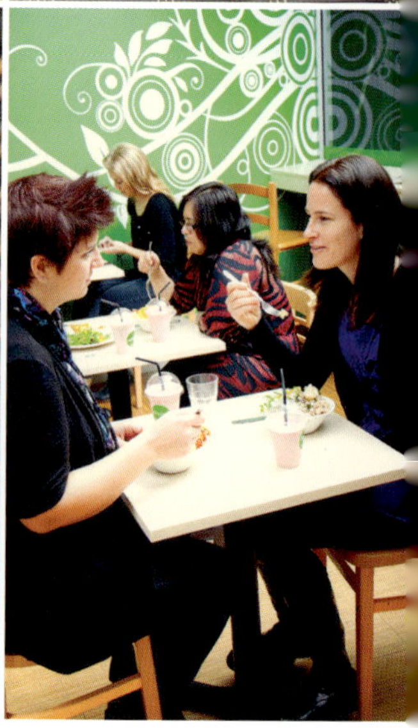
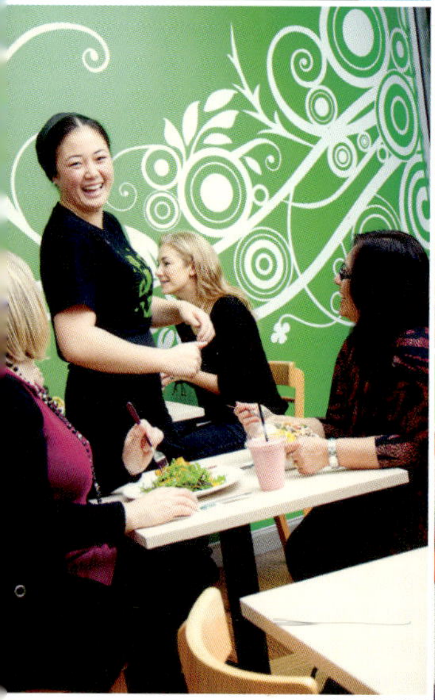
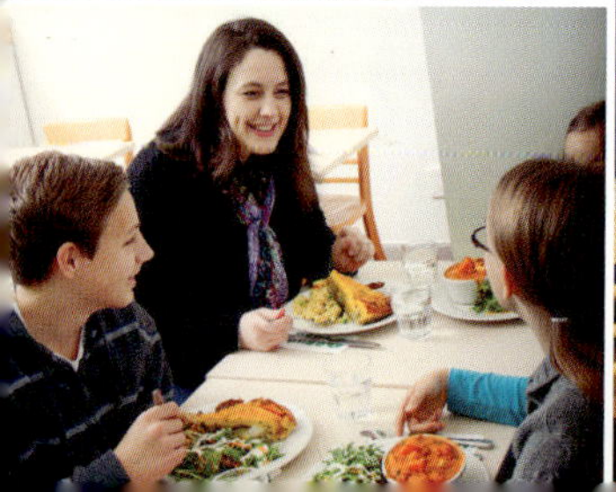
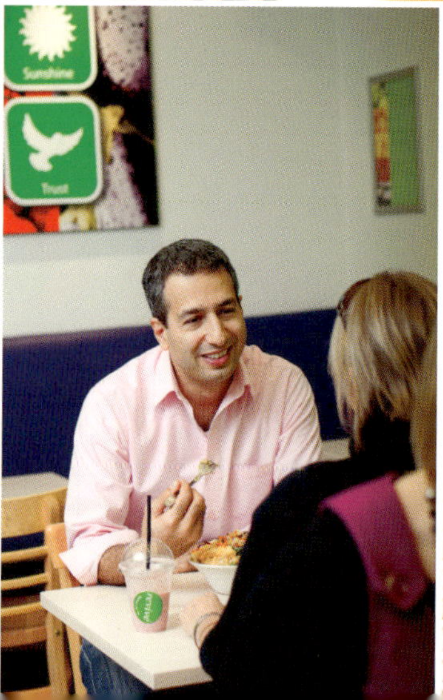
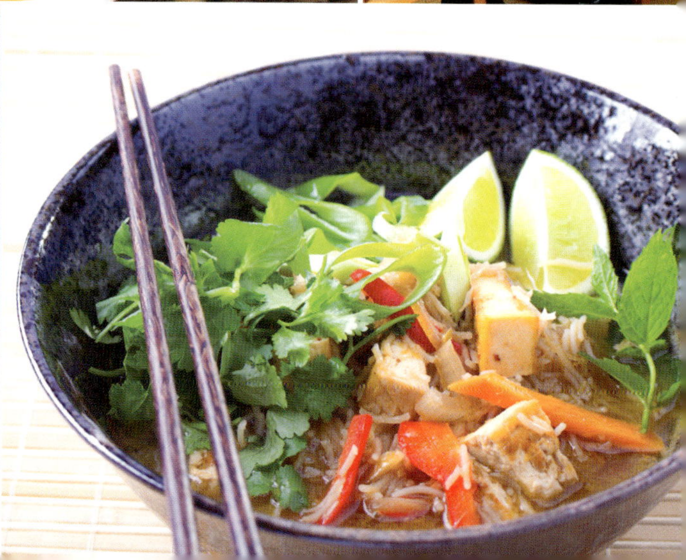

Soups

Mexican Black Bean Soup 108
Vietnamese Pho Noodles 110
Lentil & Beetroot Borscht 112
Broccoli & Dill Soup 114
Lentil & Kumara Soup 116
Leek & Potato Soup 118

I love this thick and chunky soup, however sadly it is a soup that is not very popular at Revive. Not because it is not delicious but perhaps because our basic soups like tomato and pumpkin are so amazing.

Mexican Black Bean Soup

MAKES 10 X 1 CUP SERVES

1½ cups onion finely diced (around 1 onion)

2 cloves garlic finely chopped or crushed

½ cup celery finely chopped (around 1 stalk)

1 tablespoon oil

2 x 400g (12oz) cans chopped tomatoes

3 cups hot water

2 tablespoons honey or date puree

1 teaspoon salt

2 cans (or 4 cups) cooked black beans

2 cups frozen corn

1 cup red capsicum (bell pepper) finely diced

optional ½ teaspoon finely diced chillies or chilli paste

garnish: fresh coriander (cilantro) roughly chopped

1. Saute the onion, garlic, celery and oil in a large pot until clear.
2. Add the tomatoes, water, honey and salt and bring to the boil.
3. Add the black beans and mix.
4. Using a stick blender blend around ¼ of the mix. You can also scoop out and blend in a blender or food processor.
5. Add corn and capsicum. Add chilli here if you like. Continue heating until just bubbling.
6. Garnish with coriander.

The blended beans, tomato and onion add a nice creaminess to the soup - however you do want the corn and capsicum to be whole.

Black Beans

Often called Black Turtle Beans these are a tasty bean used extensively in Mexican cooking. Great in soups, burritos, stews and curries. Soak overnight and they will usually cook in under half an hour.

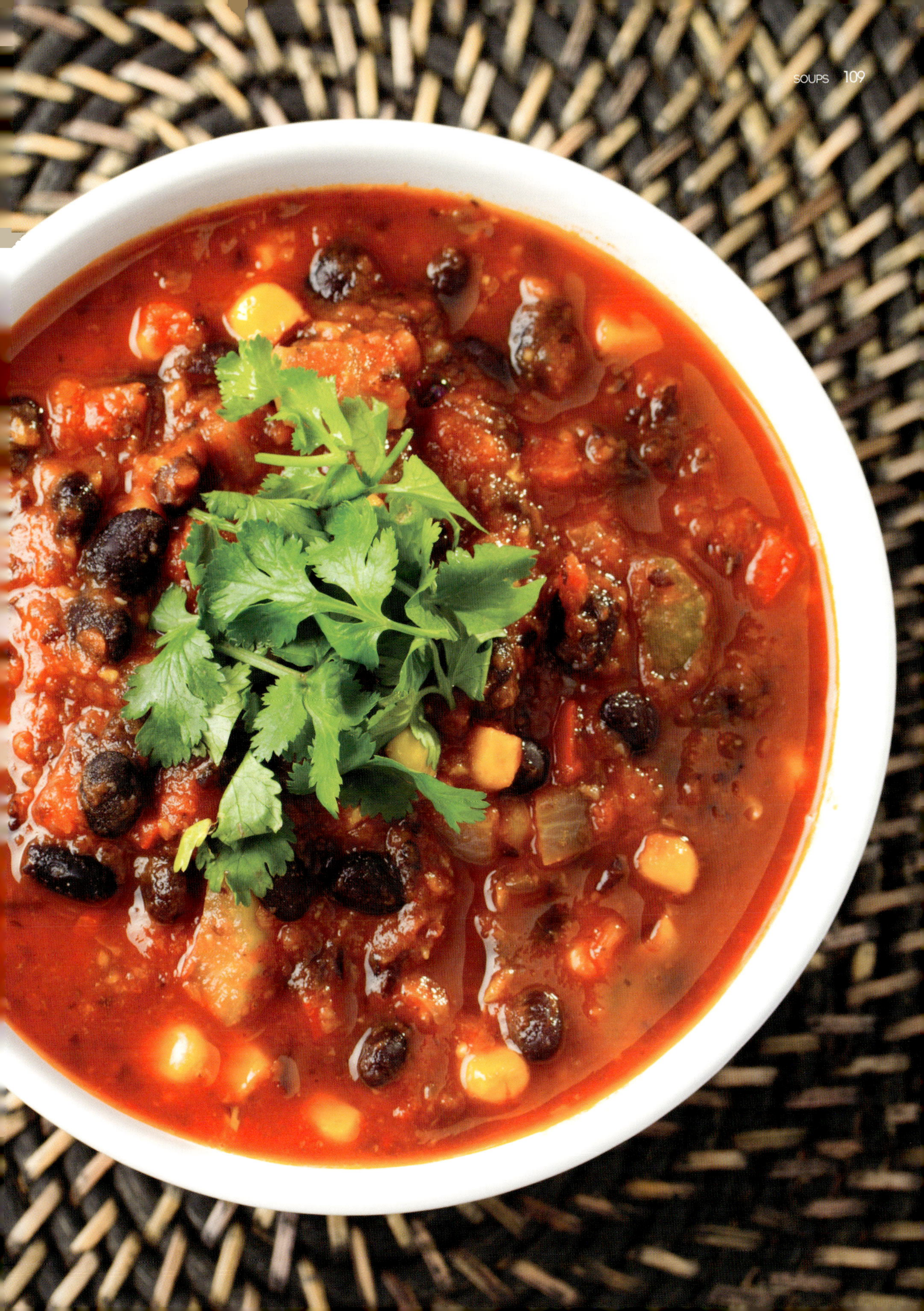

I love chunky soups with lots of ingredients and textures. In this dish the fresh herbs make a very fresh and flavoursome soup. There is something satisfying about stirring in the ingredients in to your soup as you are eating them.

Vietnamese Pho Noodles

MAKES 6 X 1 CUP SERVES

100g (3oz) thin rice noodles

2 litres (2 quarts) boiling water to cook noodles

300g (10oz) firm tofu

1 tablespoon oil

2 tablespoons soy sauce

1 tablespoon oil

1 cup onion sliced thinly (around 1 medium onion)

1 cup carrots cut into matchsticks (around 1 medium carrot)

2 tablespoons finely chopped ginger or ginger puree

¼ teaspoon star anise powder

¼ teaspoon cinnamon powder

1 teaspoon coriander powder

4 cups boiling water for soup

3 tablespoons soy sauce

½ red capsicum (bell pepper) thinly sliced

TOPPINGS

fresh coriander (cilantro) roughly chopped

lime wedges

spring onions (scallions) sliced diagonally

mint leaves

1. Put the noodles in boiling water for around 10 minutes until soft. It is not necessary to cook. Drain.

2. Slice the tofu into thick slabs and saute in a non-stick pan with the oil. Around 5 minutes per side. When golden, drizzle the soy sauce over.

3. In a pot, wok or pan saute the oil, onion, carrot and ginger until nearly soft. Add the spices at the end and stir in.

4. Add the water and soy sauce and simmer for 25 minutes with the lid on.

5. Add the capsicum, cooked tofu and drained noodles and simmer for another 5 minutes.

6. Serve the soup in a bowl and add liberal amounts of the topping ingredients – clustered in different corners of the bowl.

SOUPS 111

I was not sure whether to put this in the hotpot section or the soup section. We sell it as a hotpot at Revive, however I think it is more of a soup so it ended up in this section. This vividly red dish is amazing and has the nice earthy flavours of the beetroot and fresh flavours from the caraway seeds.

Lentil & Beetroot Borscht

MAKES 8 X 1 CUP SERVES

1½ cups onion finely sliced (around 1 onion)

2 cloves garlic finely chopped or crushed

2 tablespoons caraway seeds

1 teaspoon oil

3 cups grated beetroot (around 3 beetroot)

3 cups grated potatoes (around 2 potatoes)

3 cups grated carrot (around 3 medium carrots)

4 cups boiling water

1 can French green (puy) lentils

2 teaspoons salt

100ml (3oz) coconut cream

optional: 1 teaspoon crushed chilli paste

garnish: coriander (cilantro)

garnish: cashew cream

1. In a large pot saute the onion, garlic, seeds and oil until the onion is soft.

2. Using a hand grater or food processor, grate the beetroot, potatoes and carrots. Add to the onion mix.

3. Add water and simmer for 30 minutes.

4. Using a stick blender, blend around one third of the mixture. Alternatively take out ⅓ of the mixture and blend in a blender.

5. Stir in remaining ingredients and garnish with coriander and cashew cream.

6. Serve on rice as a main meal, or in a bowl as a soup.

This recipe calls for canned French green (puy) lentils, however you can easily cook your own or use any brownish variety.

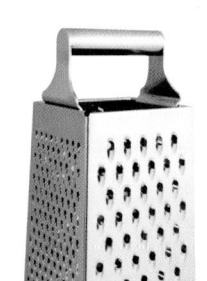

Hand Grater

An essential kitchen tool for grating vegetables. When I have a carrot or small amount of grating I just use my hand grater. When I have a large amount to grate I use the grating attachment on my food processor.

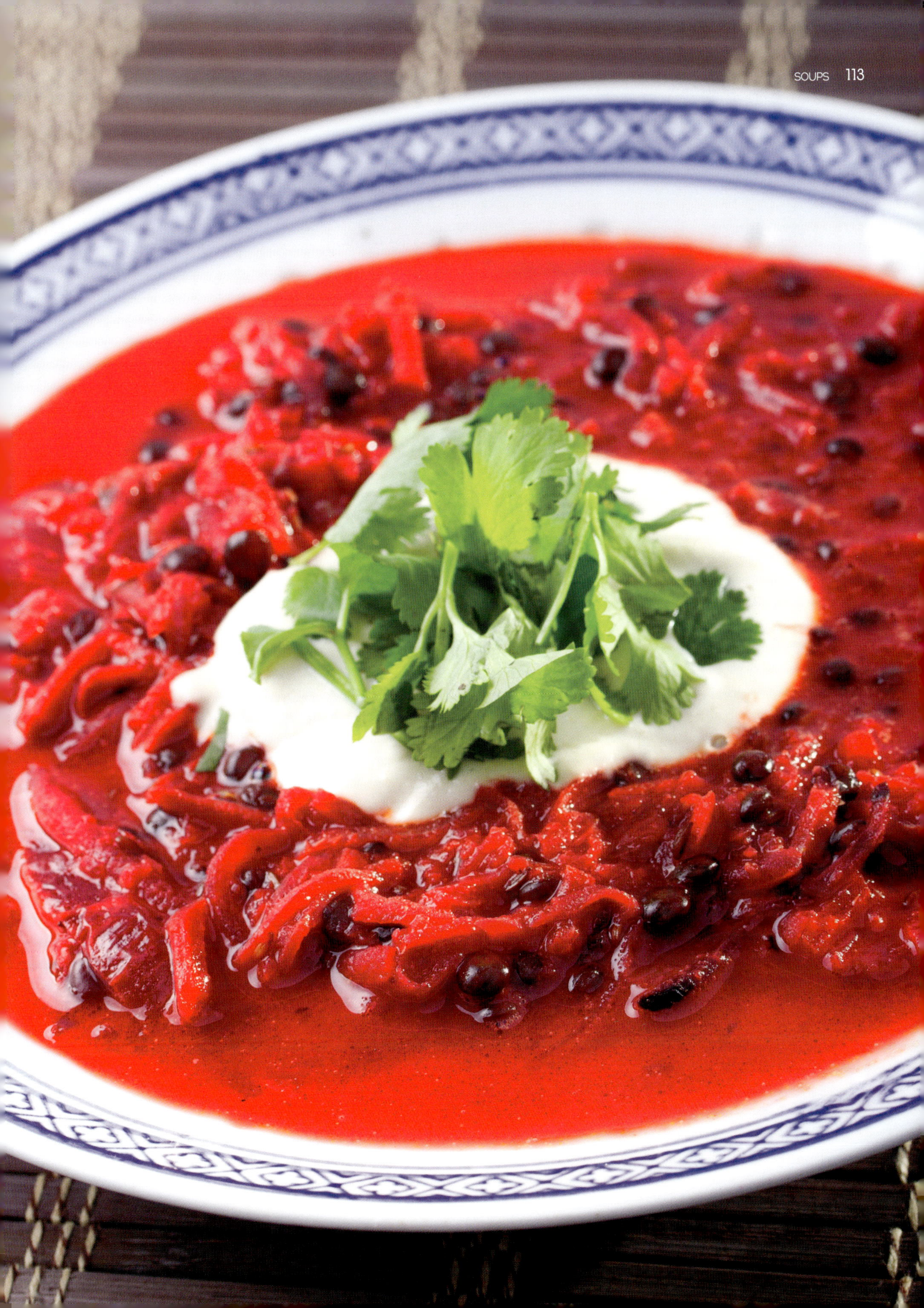

Broccoli & Dill Soup

MAKES 10 X 1 CUP SERVES

1½ cups onion diced (about 1 onion)

2 cups celery including leaves (around 2 stalks)

3 cloves garlic

1 tablespoon oil

3 cups potatoes cubed (around 2 potatoes)

5 cups water

3 teaspoons salt

3 tablespoons nutritional yeast flakes

½ cup dill finely chopped or 2 tablespoons dill paste

5 cups broccoli roughly chopped (around 1-2 heads)

1 cup sunflower seeds

1 cup water

1. In a large pot saute the onion, celery, garlic and oil until clear.
2. Add the potatoes and water and cook until potatoes are soft.
3. Add the salt, nutritional yeast flakes, dill and broccoli and cook for around 1 minute or until broccoli is slightly soft. You want the broccoli to be only briefly cooked so it retains its colour.
4. Blend with a stick blender.
5. With a blender or stick blender blend the sunflower seeds and water until you have a cream. Mix in with the soup.
6. Serve with some cashew cream swirled around on top.

Use all the celery including leaves, and the broccoli stalks (just discard the tough end pieces).

Serving Bowls

Having a range of large bowls to serve hotpots and soups is great. Check out a Japanese grocery store for some great bowls. These stores usually have a good range of nice bowls that you will make your food look great.

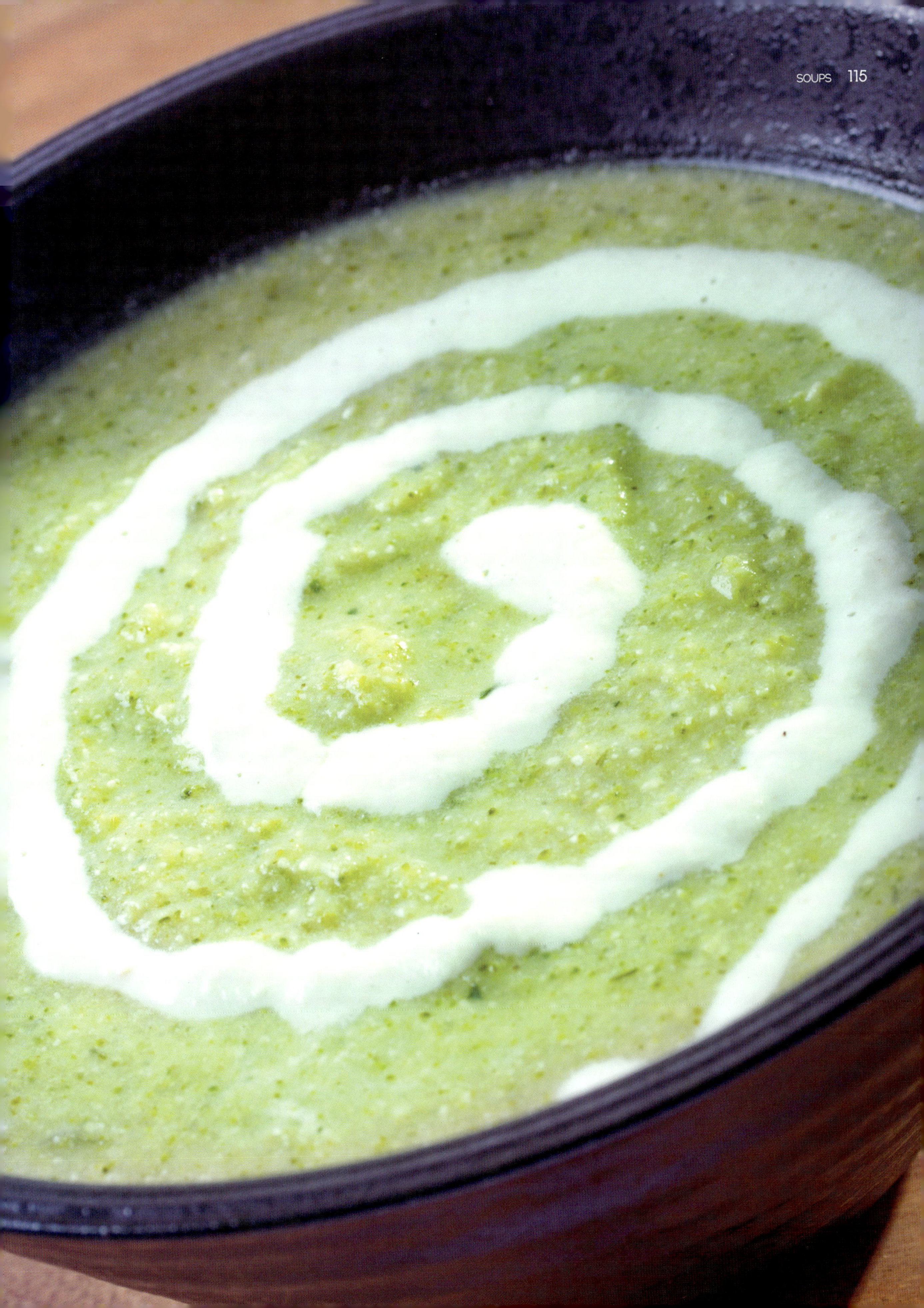

This soup has lovely flavours, the kumara makes it go nice and thick, and the lime juice adds a subtle pacific flavour.

Lentil & Kumara Soup

MAKES 8 X 1 CUP SERVES

1½ cups onions diced (around 1 onion)

1 cup celery diced (around 2 stalks)

1 tablespoon chopped ginger or ginger puree

1 tablespoon oil

1 teaspoon turmeric powder

2 teaspoons mild curry powder

5 cups boiling water

1 cup red lentils

3 cups red kumara (sweet potato) un-peeled and cubed (around 2 kumara)

1½ teaspoons salt

200ml (6oz) coconut cream

juice of 2 limes

garnish: parsley

1. Saute onions, celery, ginger and oil in a pot until onion is clear.
2. Add spices and mix for around 30 seconds.
3. Add water, lentils and kumara and simmer for around 15 minutes or until lentils are soft and kumara is cooked.
4. Blend with a stick blender.
5. Mix in remaining ingredients and serve garnished with parsley.

Do not add salt until the end as it can inhibit the lentils cooking properly.

This is a very thick soup, however you can add water to thin it down if you like it runnier.

SOUPS 117

This is the smoothest and loveliest soup. Possibly not your traditional leek and potato soup but a more flavoursome variation.

Leek & Potato Soup

MAKES 8 X 1 CUP SERVES

3 cups leeks sliced thinly (around 1 large leek)

1½ cups onions diced (around 1 onion)

2 cups celery chopped (around 2 large stalks)

2 cups carrot diced (around 1 large carrot)

2 cloves garlic finely chopped or crushed

1 tablespoon oil

½ teaspoon nutmeg

4 cups boiling water

5 cups potatoes cubed (about 4 potatoes)

1½ teaspoons salt

1 cup cold water

1 cup cashews

1 pinch cayenne pepper

2 tablespoons honey or date puree

garnish: chives

garnish: cashew cream

1. In a large pot saute the leeks, onion, celery, carrot and garlic in the oil until clear.

2. Add nutmeg and stir briefly.

3. Add water, potatoes and salt. Bring to the boil and simmer covered for around 10 minutes or until the potatoes are soft.

4. Using a potato masher, mash the mixture until there are no chunks of potato.

5. Using a stick blender, blend ¼ of the mixture so you create a thick soup and also retain the chunks of vegetables. You can also use a blender/liquidiser to blend.

6. In a separate container, blend the cold water and cashews together to form a cashew cream.

7. Add cashew cream (reserve a little for garnish) and remaining ingredients to the pot and bring back to heat.

8. Serve with a swirl of the remaining cashew cream and some chives.

Potato Masher

This is a great tool when you want to make some large vegetables mingle into a soup while still keeping some texture. Often just a quick press or two is all that is required.

SOUPS 119

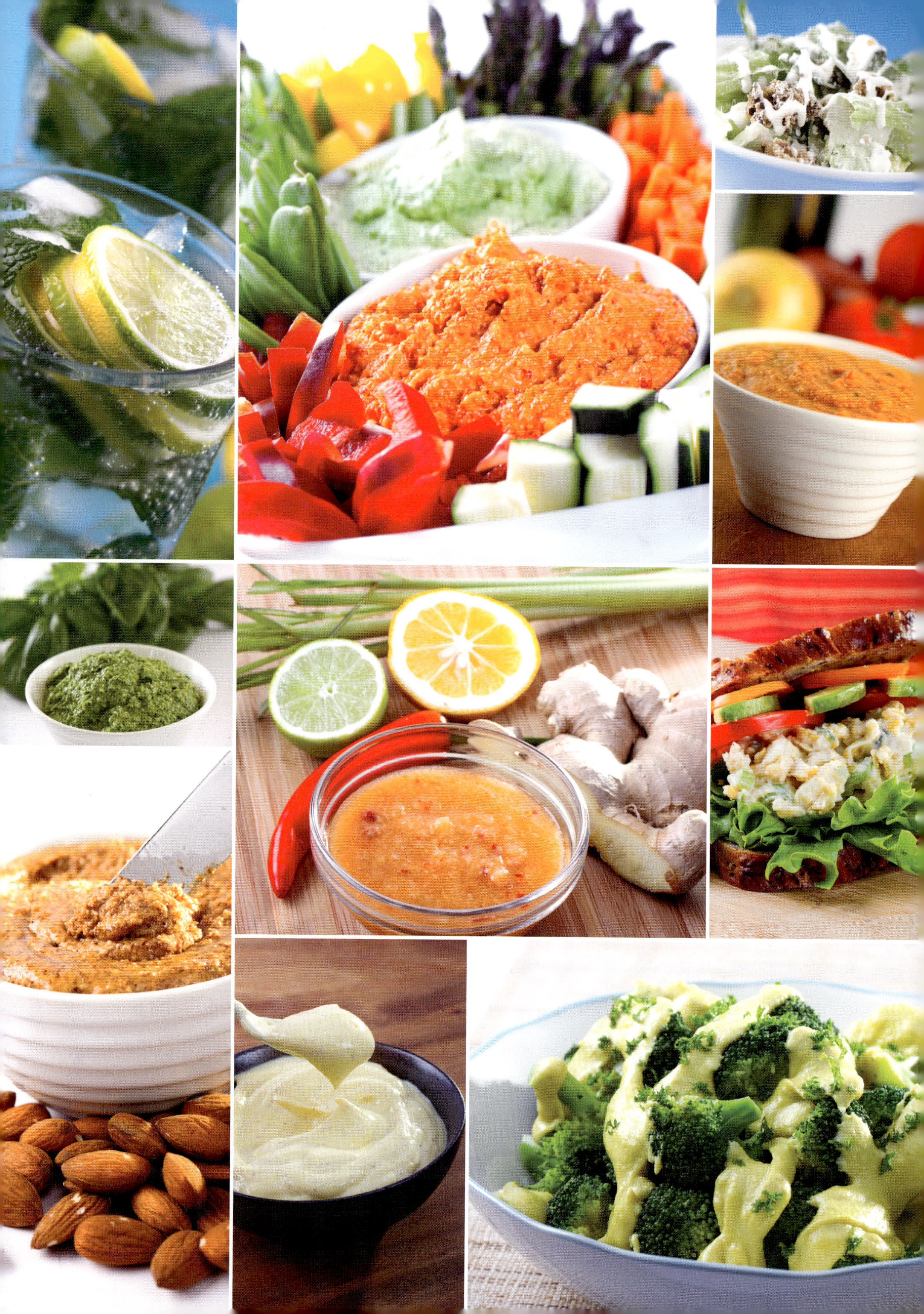

Flavour Boosters

- Cheezy Cashew Sauce 122
- Basil Hummus 124
- Nutty Capsicum Dip 124
- Sparkling Lime Juice 126
- Almost Egg Spread 128
- Thai Ginger Dressing 130
- Tofu Mayo 132
- Almond Butter 133
- Revive Aioli 134
- Italian Tomato Sauce 134
- Basil Pesto 135
- Date Puree 135

Cheese sauce can transform steamed vegetables, however the traditional recipe with milk, butter, cheese and white flour is not helpful in keeping good health. Try this great recipe for making your steamed vegetables taste awesome!

Cheezy Cashew Sauce

MAKES 2 CUPS

¼ teaspoon salt

1 tablespoon nutritional yeast flakes

1 cup cashew nuts raw

1¼ cups water

¼ teaspoon turmeric powder

½ teaspoon arrowroot or cornflour

1. Put all ingredients into a blender or liquidiser and blend until smooth. You may have to add a little more water.

2. Pour into a pot or non-stick frying pan and heat while stirring until desired thickness is achieved.

3. Serve over steamed vegetables.

The thickening process will happen quite quickly so do not get distracted.

Nutritional yeast flakes are not always stocked at supermarkets so you may need to visit a health or whole foods store.

Blender/Liquidiser

This is an essential kitchen tool for making dressings, smoothies and sauces. It is useful for when the ingredients will stay liquid. For thick or solid items you will need a food processor which is larger and has a S blade. A stick blender is a good alternative if you do not have a blender.

FLAVOUR BOOSTERS 123

I love dips. There are some great dipping vegetables around such as asparagus, courgettes (zucchini), sugar snap peas, capsicum (bell pepper) in 4 colours, and carrots. These dips will usually last around 2-3 days in the refrigerator.

Basil Hummus

MAKES 2 CUPS

2 x 400g (12oz) cans of chickpeas (garbanzo beans)

1 cup (pressed down) fresh basil

½ teaspoon of salt

2 cloves of garlic chopped or crushed

3 tablespoons tahini (ground hulled sesame seed paste)

¼ cup water

4 tablespoons lemon juice

1. Put all ingredients in food processor and blend until smooth. You can also use a stick blender or a regular blender however you may have to add more water to keep it flowing.

2. Taste. All batches of hummus vary in flavour as salt, chickpeas and lemon juice always have different flavours and consistency.

3. Add any extra water, tahini or salt as needed. You should be able to taste every ingredient slightly, with not too much of any ingredient dominating.

Serve with fresh sliced vegetables for dipping.

Nutty Capsicum Dip

MAKES 1½ CUPS

1 cup cashew nuts raw

4 cloves garlic roughly chopped or crushed

1 tablespoon oil

2 red capsicum (bell pepper) roughly chopped

¾ teaspoon salt

2 tablespoons lemon juice

1. In a hot pan saute the cashew nuts, garlic, oil and capsicum for around 5 minutes or until the capsicum is soft. This will smell amazing!

2. Add the salt and lemon juice and tip into a blender and blend for 1 minute or until smooth. You may have to add a little water to achieve a blending consistency.

For a crunchier texture, add ¼ cup of cashew nuts at the end to the blender and blend for a couple of seconds so you get small pieces in the dip.

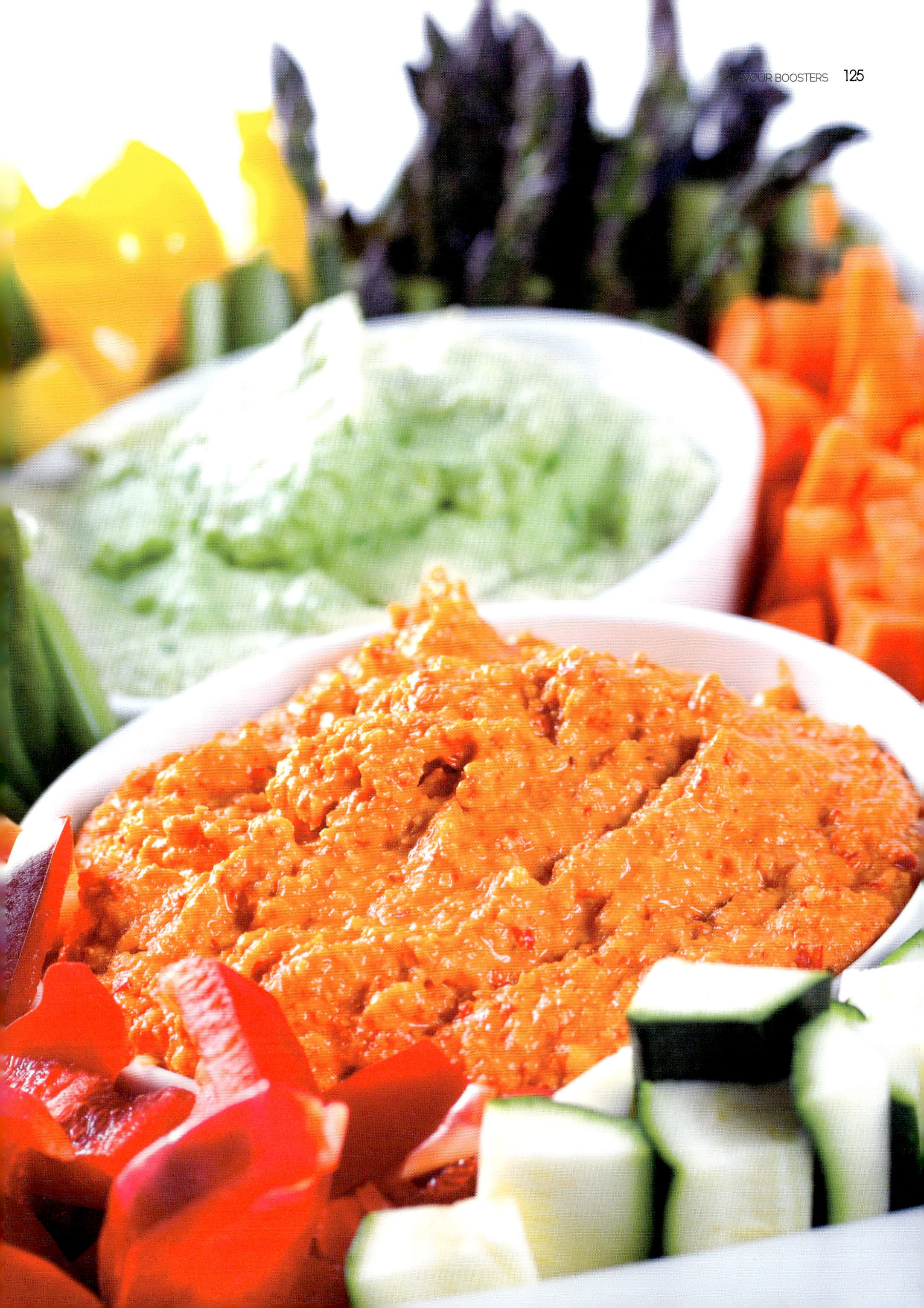

This is a new favourite drink of mine. It has a subtle flavour, is refreshing and quick to make. And without any sugar!

Sparkling Lime Juice

MAKES 2 X 2 CUP SERVES

juice of ½ lime

10 mint leaves

8 large cubes of ice

sliced lemon and lime

1 litre (32 oz) soda water or sparkling mineral water

1. Squeeze juice into a glass.
2. Add mint, ice and sliced lemon and lime.
3. Pour the sparkling water into the glass.

You can also use other citrus fruits like lemons, oranges or grapefruits.

If you want a mintier flavour, bruise the mint or crunch it in your hands before adding.

Ice Cubes

A great addition to most drinks and smoothies. And the cost is free! Good to have on hand so be prepared and re-stock your ice when you use it.

FLAVOUR BOOSTERS 127

I was looking to make a healthy sandwich one Sunday and combined a couple of recipes to make this. I was surprised how good it tasted. The best part about making a cookbook is that I get to eat most of the recipes I photograph!

Almost Egg Spread

MAKES 3 CUPS

400g can chickpeas (garbanzo beans) mashed

1 cup tofu mayo (page 132)

1 cup celery (around 2 stalks) finely diced

½ cup finely chopped spring onions (scallions) (around 2 stalks)

1 teaspoon lemon juice

½ teaspoon salt

SANDWICH COMPONENTS:

whole grain bread

tomatoes

lettuce

avocado

capsicum (bell peppers)

1. Mix the ingredients together.

2. Make a sandwich with some whole grain bread, salad vegetables and the "almost egg" spread.

This filling will keep in the refrigerator for around 2 days so consume quickly.

FLAVOUR BOOSTERS 129

This dressing is a lovely way to experience Thai flavours in a salad. We use it in our Thai Coleslaw. You can make it in advance (up to 2 weeks) and just keep it in the refrigerator and add to any salad. It will also work in a curry if you want some extra zing!

Thai Ginger Dressing

MAKES ¾ CUP

2 tablespoons ginger puree

2 tablespoons lemon juice

1 tablespoon lime juice

2 tablespoons lemongrass very finely diced

2 tablespoons honey

½ teaspoon chilli puree or finely chopped red chillies

1 teaspoon salt

2 tablespoons oil

1. Put all ingredients into a mixing bowl or dressing shaker and mix. This dressing does not need blending.

You can buy lemongrass frozen and pre-chopped from Asian supermarkets. This works well however you will need twice the amount as it is not as flavoursome as fresh.

For a hotter dressing add more chilli.

You can use chilli powder or cayenne pepper instead of chilli puree, however you will need significantly less. A pinch will be sufficient depending on how hot your powder is.

FLAVOUR BOOSTERS 131

This is a great low fat alternative. It can be used instead of aioli or mayonnaise. It is easy to make and has a similar creamy texture to aioli.

Tofu Mayo

MAKES 2 CUPS

2 cups (350g/10oz) firm tofu

5 tablespoons lemon juice

1 tablespoon whole-grain mustard

1 clove garlic

1 tablespoon honey or date puree

1 teaspoon salt

1. Put all ingredients into a blender, food processor or use a stick blender and blend until smooth.

2. If it is too thick and stalls the blender you can add a little more water.

You can also add a little turmeric if you want a more yellow colour.

As this contains fresh tofu, this will keep in the refrigerator for only a couple of days so use up quickly.

This is a great alternative to peanut butter

Almond Butter

MAKES 2 CUPS

2 cups raw almonds

2 tablespoons oil

1 teaspoon salt

1. Put the almonds on a baking tray and bake in the oven for 8 minutes at 180°C (350°F).

2. Allow to cool for 5 minutes.

3. Put the almonds, oil and salt into a food processor and blend.

4. When blending, it will start out as a crumbly texture. After around 2 minutes will start to clump up as the nuts release their oils, and will suddenly become almond butter.

Store in the refrigerator. It will last at least a month or more.

You may need to stir each time as the oils will separate due to the lack of any chemical stabilisers usually found in nut butters.

Revive Aioli

MAKES 3 CUPS

½ cup soy milk

1 tablespoon cider vinegar or lemon juice

3 cloves garlic

1 tablespoon whole-grain mustard

½ teaspoon salt

2 cups oil

½ to 1 cup room temperature water

1. Select a blender, food processor or stick blender.
2. Blend all ingredients (except oil and water).
3. While blending, slowly add oil and then add water at end until desired consistency is reached.

When making dressings you need to ensure that all items are at room temperature, and that you add the oil slowly.

Aioli will last 2-3 weeks in your refrigerator.

Italian Tomato Sauce

MAKES 6 CUPS

1½ cups onion roughly chopped (around 1 onion)

4 cloves garlic crushed

2 tablespoons oil

3 x 400g (14oz) cans tomatoes

¾ teaspoon salt

1 teaspoon mixed dried herbs

3 tablespoons honey or date puree

1. In a pot saute onion, garlic and oil until clear.
2. Add remaining ingredients and cook until bubbling.
3. Blend all the sauce with a stick blender.

If you really like garlic add twice as much for a great garlic taste.

FLAVOUR BOOSTERS 135

Basil Pesto

MAKES 2 CUPS

1 large bunch fresh basil (around 125g/4oz)

½ cup rice bran oil

1 cup raw cashew nuts

½ teaspoon salt

¼ cup lemon juice (around 2 lemons)

2 cloves garlic

1. Put all ingredients into a food processor and blend until it is well mixed, but there are still some nut pieces showing.

2. You can use a blender or stick blender but you will have to add a little more oil or water to make the mixture turn.

For a different flavour you can use almonds or walnuts instead of cashew nuts.

Traditionally pesto uses pine nuts - however these are around 4 times the price of almonds and cashews.

Use coriander (cilantro) instead of basil for a different pesto.

Date Puree

MAKES 2 CUPS

2 cups pitted dried dates

2 cups boiling water

1. Put dates in boiling water for 5 minutes to soften.

2. Put the water and dates in blender and blend well until you have a smooth paste.

3. If you hear date stones (as they occasionally come through), sieve the puree.

4. Put into an air-tight container and store in the refrigerator. Will last at least 3 weeks.

You can use cold water to soak the dates - however it will take several hours for them to soften.

Date puree will last 2-3 weeks in your refrigerator.

THE RECIPES ON THESE PAGES HAVE BEEN REPEATED FROM "THE REVIVE CAFE COOKBOOK 1 & 2"

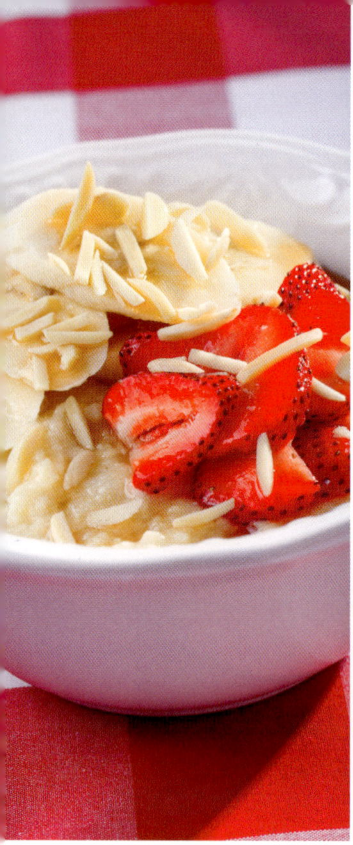
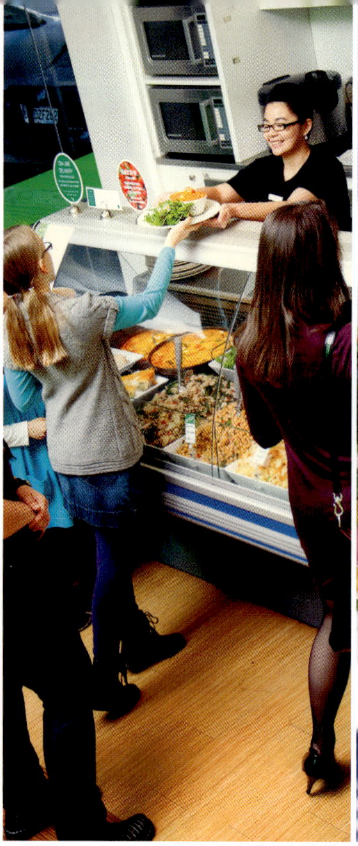
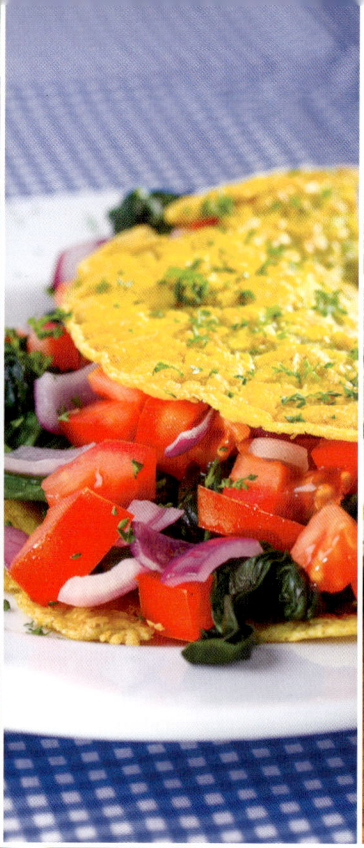
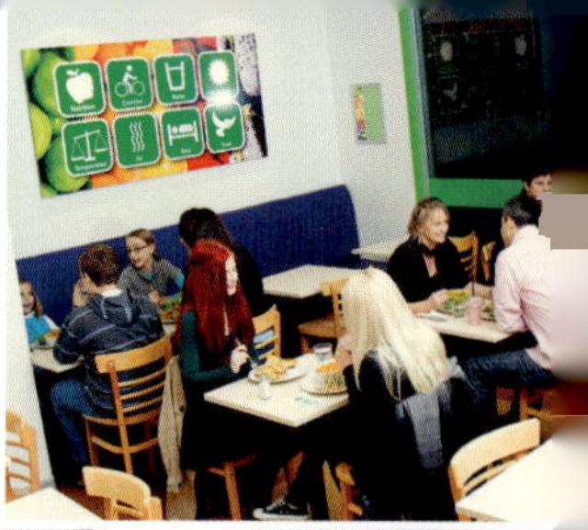
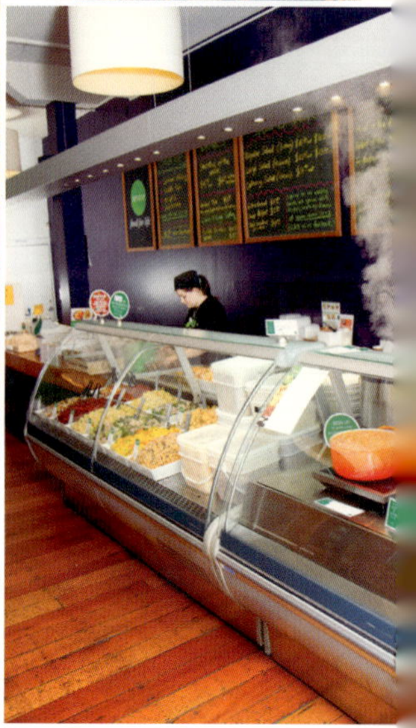
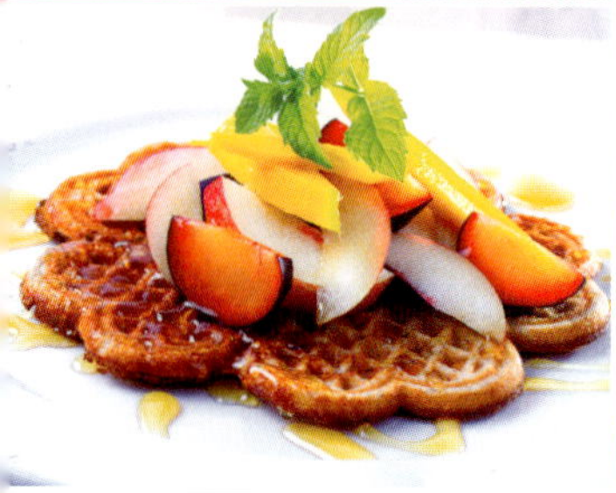
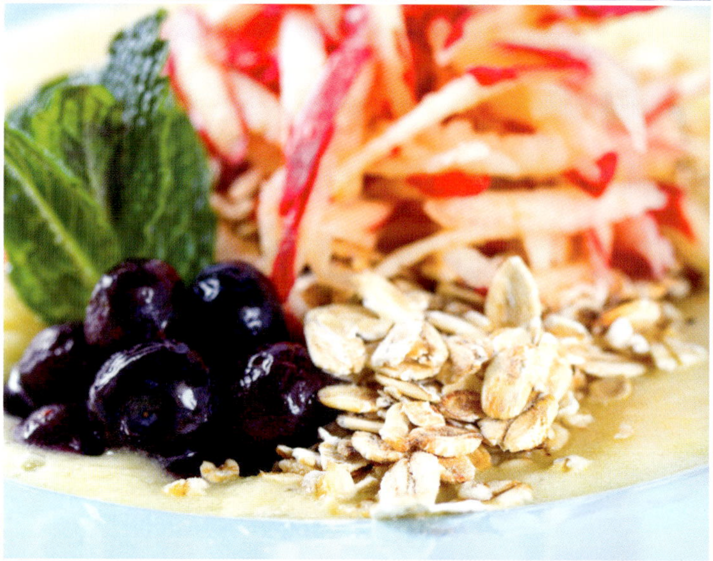
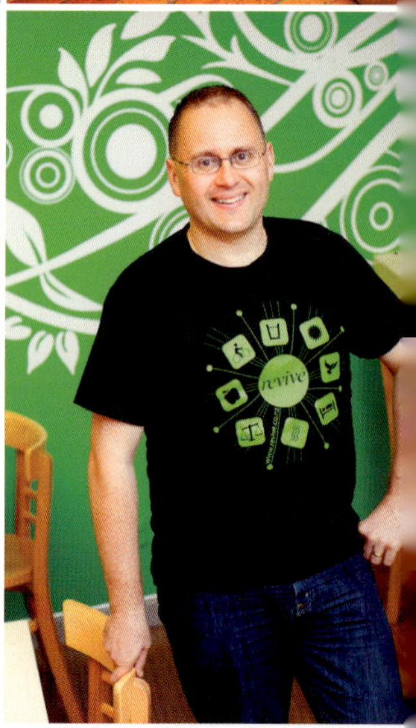
revive
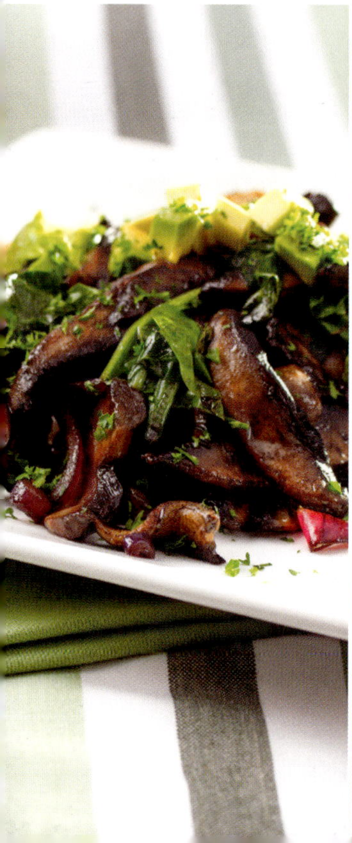
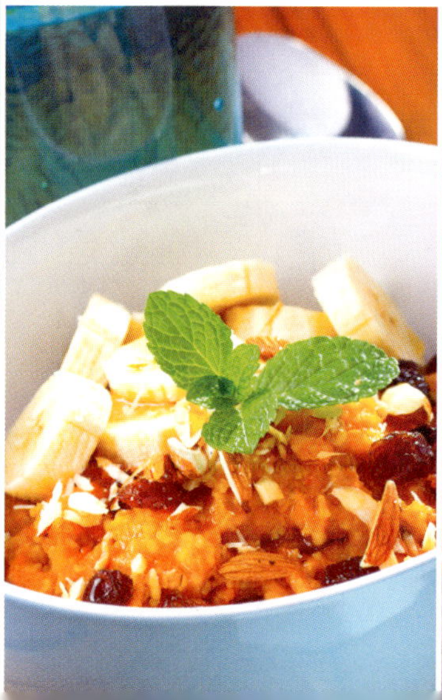
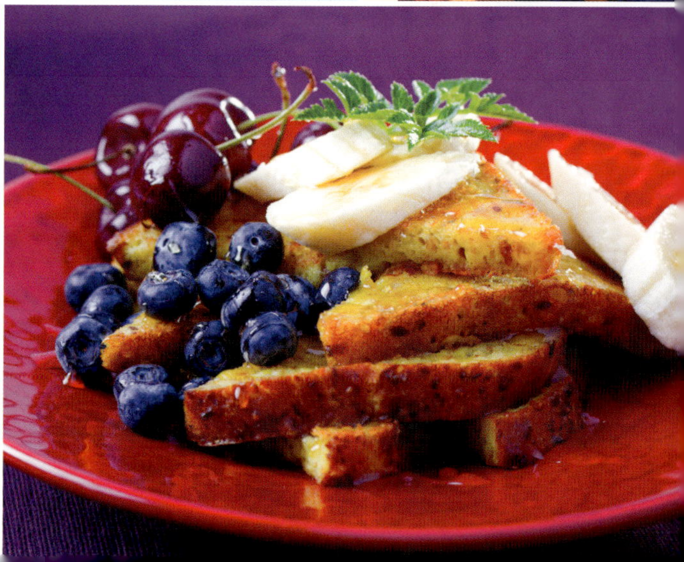

Breakfasts

Power Oat Breakfast	138
Nearly French Toast	140
Warming Millet Porridge	142
Buckwheat Waffles	144
Butternut Oatmeal	146
Golden Omelette	148
Portobello Mushrooms	150

This is a great breakfast you can use if you want a simpler lifestyle for a week. Similar recipes are often used in fasts or cleansing diets. However this is still very delicious.

Power Oat Breakfast

SERVES 2

1 frozen banana

1 cup pineapple juice

1 cup jumbo (whole) rolled oats

1 cup frozen blueberries

1 apple grated

1. In a blender, add the banana and pineapple juice and blend so you have a creamy mixture.

2. In a hot pan, dry toast the oats for around 3 minutes or until they start curling.

3. Prepare the fruit.

4. Pour the pineapple banana mixture into a bowl and serve the oats and fruit on top.

You can use chopped or quick rolled oats if you do not have jumbo.

Use other fresh or frozen fruits like strawberries, mangoes, pears or plums.

Grated Apple

I love grated apple. It is so fresh and crunchy without too much chewing required. It is great on breakfasts and in salads too. Use a normal hand grater to grate but note it will turn brown quickly so you have to eat straight away or mix with other ingredients.

BREAKFASTS 139

I found some non-egg French toast recipes and modified to come up with this one. I did not believe it would be possible however these taste amazing. They also go especially well with berries (which have a sour side to them) and the sweet honey.

Nearly French Toast

MAKES 8 SLICES

1 cup water
¼ cup raw cashew nuts
½ teaspoon vanilla essence
1 tablespoon honey
⅛ teaspoon turmeric
¼ teaspoon salt
8 slices whole-grain bread

TOPPINGS:

fresh fruit (cherries, blueberries, strawberries, boysenberries)
honey or maple syrup

1. Put all ingredients (except the bread) in a blender (or use a stick blender) and blend until it is smooth.
2. Cut the bread in half diagonally (you will have 16 pieces total).
3. Pour into a bowl and dip the bread into the cashew mix for a couple of seconds to completely coat the bread.
4. Heat a non-stick frying pan. Depending on the quality of your pan, you may be able to get away with using no oil at all. Or you may wish to use a couple of drops to start with.
5. Cook for around 2 minutes per side.
6. Serve immediately with fresh berries and a drizzle of honey or maple syrup.

Make sure you blend the mixture really well so you have a consistent paste rather than water with little cashew bits.

Vanilla Essence

For a delicate taste to round out many sweet dishes, vanilla essence is great. Just put a couple of drops in. You can of course use vanilla bean pods for a truly authentic flavour however these are very expensive.

BREAKFASTS 141

This is my wife Verity's favourite breakfast. It is light yet filling and nutritious. Millet is not just bird seed, it is a nutritious grain and makes an excellent breakfast.

Warming Millet Porridge

MAKES 2 SERVES

½ cup finely ground millet

⅛ teaspoon salt

2 cups cold water

TOPPINGS

fresh fruit

maple syrup or honey

chopped nuts

1. Mix all ingredients in a pot and heat quickly while stirring.
2. When mixture is bubbling cook for around a minute more.
3. Serve with breakfast toppings.

You can make the cooking process faster by mixing a little cold water with the millet and then adding boiling water for the rest.

Millet

Millet is an excellent whole grain and is not just for birds. You can buy as flour or grind into flour yourself using a coffee grinder.

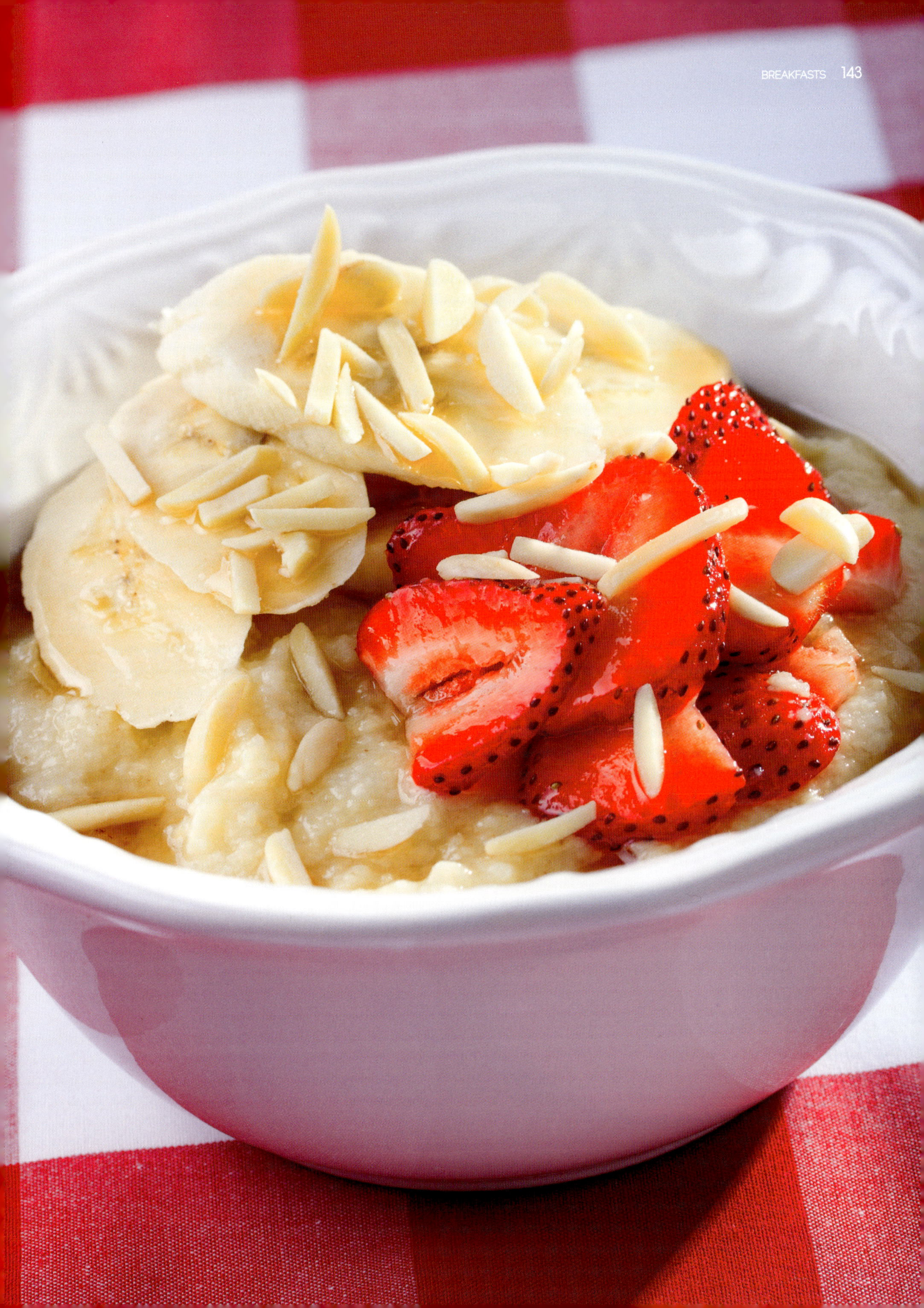

One Sunday morning I felt like a romantic breakfast with my wife. I dusted off my waffle maker and tried out several recipes and came up with this winner. It is great with summer fruits and a drizzle of honey.

Buckwheat Waffles

MAKES 5 WAFFLES

1 cup buckwheat flour

¼ cup potato flour (sometimes called potato starch)

½ cup brown rice flour

½ teaspoon salt

1½ cups rice milk

2 tablespoons honey

2 tablespoons oil

TOPPINGS:

fresh summer fruit

drizzle of honey or maple syrup

1. Sift dry ingredients into a bowl.
2. Add wet ingredients and mix until you have a smooth batter.
3. Heat and lightly oil your waffle iron before each waffle.
4. Pour ½ cup of mixture in and cook for 5 minutes.
5. Serve immediately and garnish with fresh fruit and a drizzle of honey or maple syrup.

You can make your own buckwheat flour in a coffee grinder.

Potato flour is usually found in health food stores or bulk stores.

Buckwheat Flour

A great grain that has a nice nutty taste. Good in breakfasts and in waffles. Buy as flour or you can grind it yourself in a coffee grinder.

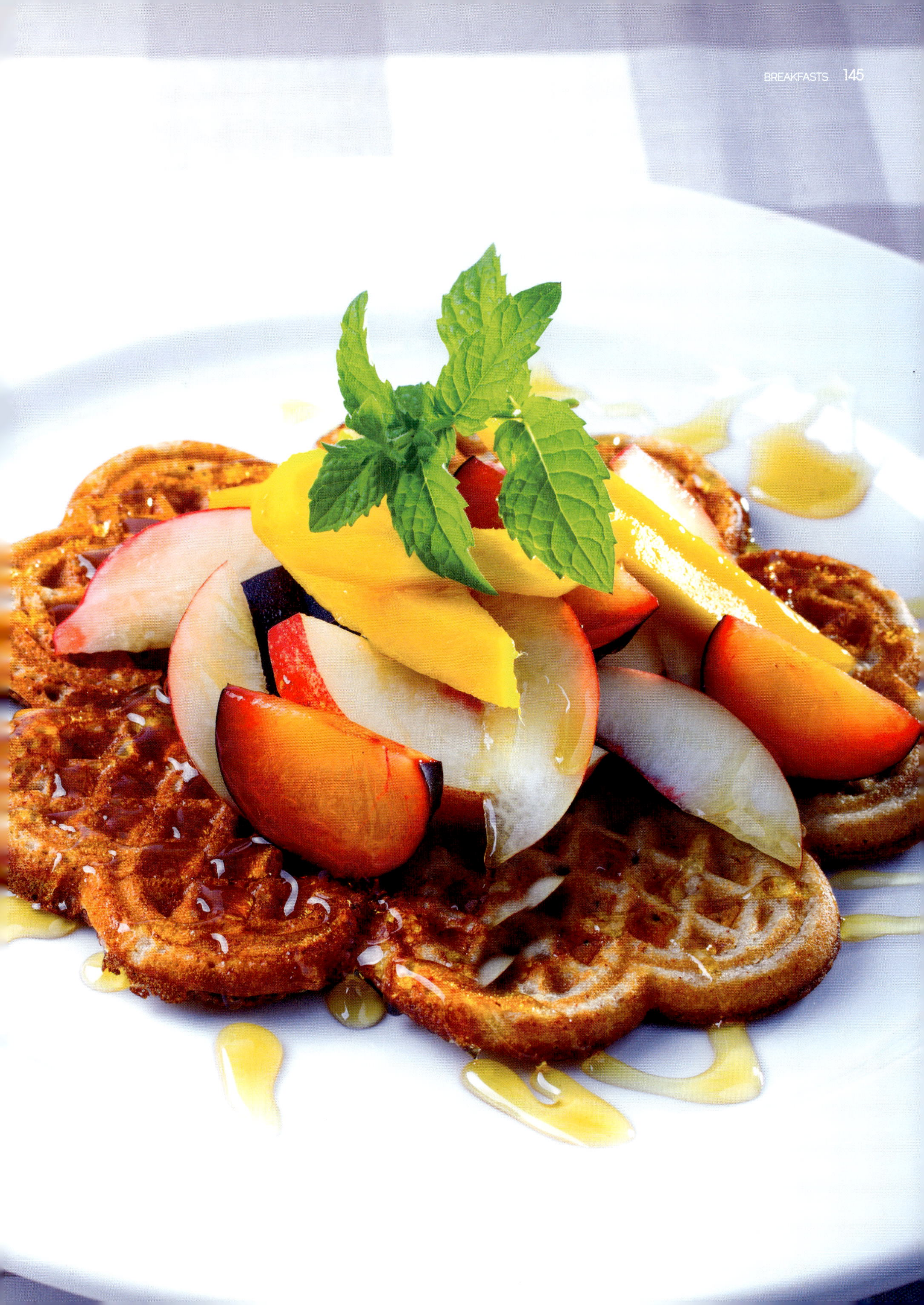

Mel, who is on my team at Revive, suggested this dish. I gave it a try and it was excellent. It is something different but just think pumpkin pie for breakfast and that should put your taste buds in the right space.

Butternut Oatmeal

MAKE 2 X 1 CUP SERVES

1½ cups butternut or pumpkin de-skinned and cubed

½ cup rolled oats

¾ cup water

½ cup rice, soy or almond milk

¼ teaspoon salt

2 tablespoons honey

¼ teaspoon nutmeg

TOPPINGS

sliced banana or other fruit

slivered almonds

sultanas

milk of your choice

honey drizzled over

1. Brush pumpkin with a little oil and roast for 15 minutes at 180°C (350°F) or until very soft.
2. In a pot add the oats, water, milk, salt. Heat well until bubbling and it is like porridge/oatmeal texture.
3. Mash pumpkin and add to porridge mixture with remaining ingredients. Mix well.
4. Serve with toppings.

You may need to add more water to achieve the desired consistency.

Butternut Pumpkin

A sweet variant of the common pumpkin. Just scoop out the seeds and roast or boil. The skin is quite soft so you can roast and eat the skin. Can be used instead of pumpkin.

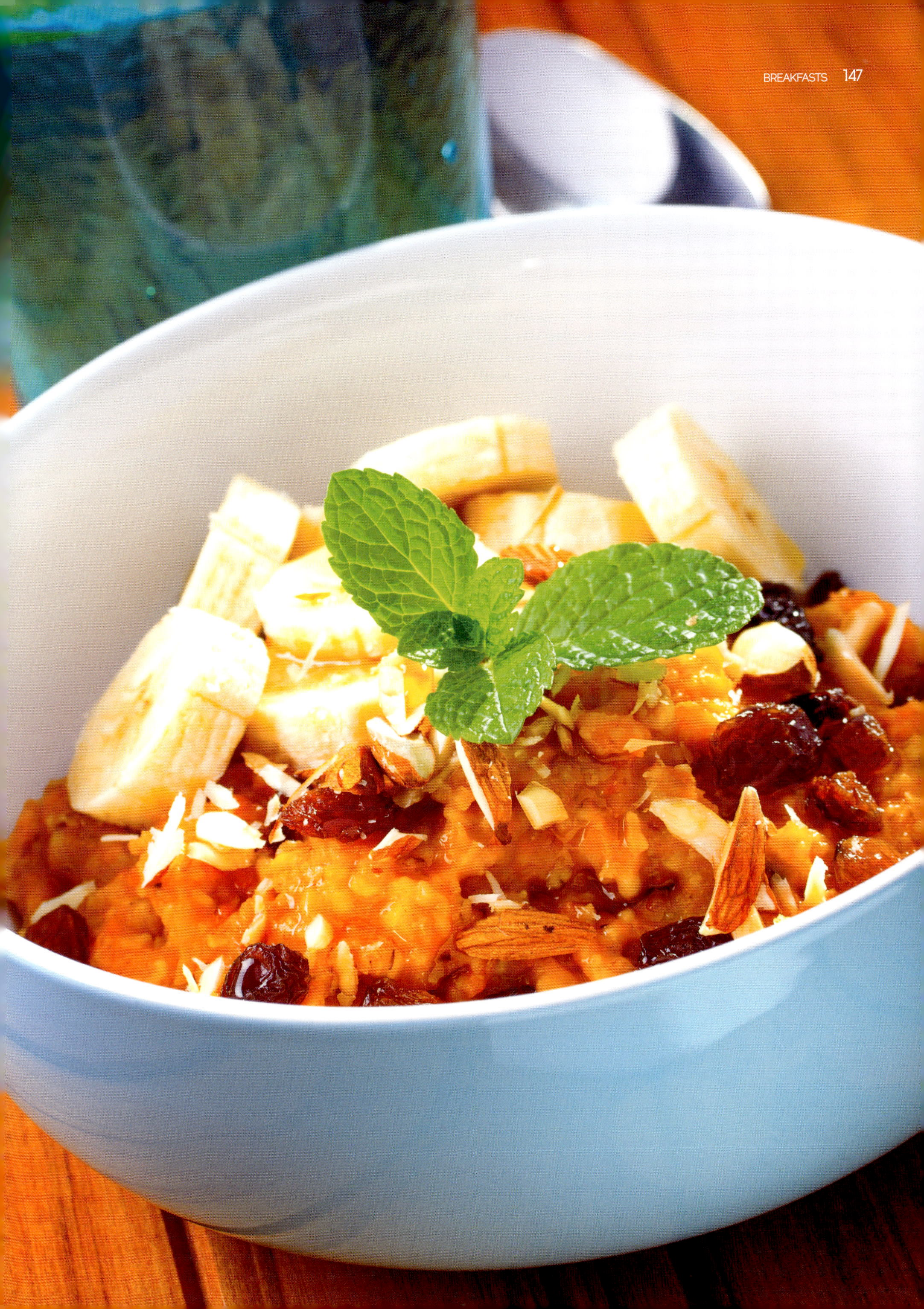

Believe it or not but you can make an omelette without eggs! Give this recipe a go if you do not believe me.

Golden Omelette

MAKES 5 OMELETTES

- 300g (10oz) firm tofu (around 1 cup)
- 1 cup oats
- 1¼ cup water
- ¼ teaspoon turmeric
- ½ teaspoon onion powder
- ¼ teaspoon garlic powder
- 1 teaspoon salt

FILLING OPTIONS CHOOSE 2-3

- 1 red onion lightly sauted
- 2 chopped tomatoes
- fresh spinach lightly steamed or frozen spinach defrosted
- 1 red capsicum (bell pepper) sliced
- 100g (3oz) sauteed button mushrooms

1. Put ingredients into blender and blend until smooth.
2. Allow to sit for around 5 minutes for oats to soften and then blend again.
3. Put a little oil in a hot non-stick pan and scoop in ½ cup measures.
4. Cook for around 4 minutes per side.
5. Put your choice of fillings on one half of the omelette and fold over. Slide it off the pan onto your plate.

When cooking meals like this in a frying pan the first one in is usually a test meal so I can adjust the heat and mixture consistency if necessary.

Omelette Pan

These little non-stick frying pans are excellent to have around and make great one-serve omelettes. They are good if you want to quickly saute some onions for another dish. And they pop straight into the dishwasher for easy cleaning.

BREAKFASTS 149

I will often get up early on a Sunday morning and experiment with new dishes in my kitchen at home. One Sunday morning I was cooking this dish and Verity came down the stairs and said "what's cooking, that smells awesome!" As she does not like mushrooms she was extremely disappointed when she found out what the dish actually contained.

Portobello Mushrooms

MAKES 2 X 1 CUP SERVES

- 4 flat portobello mushrooms sliced
- 1 clove garlic finely chopped or crushed
- ½ cup red onion sliced
- 1 tablespoon oil
- 6 large fresh spinach leaves
- ¼ teaspoon salt
- whole grain bread
- garnish: ¼ avocado diced finely
- garnish: parsley finely chopped

1. Saute the mushrooms, garlic, onion and oil in a pan for around 10 minutes. Put the lid on so they can sweat. Stir regularly.
2. Add the spinach leaves and salt and cook for around 1 minute so they wilt slightly.
3. Serve on whole grain bread.
4. Garnish with avocado and parsley.

If spinach is not in season you can use silverbeet (Swiss chard) or Asian greens.

This recipe would also work well with button mushrooms.

Portobello Mushrooms

Also called flat mushrooms, these big mushrooms have lots of flavour. Often just one large mushroom can be enough for a meal. Saute them whole or sliced. Sweating mushrooms helps the flavour, so put a lid on while cooking.

BREAKFASTS 151

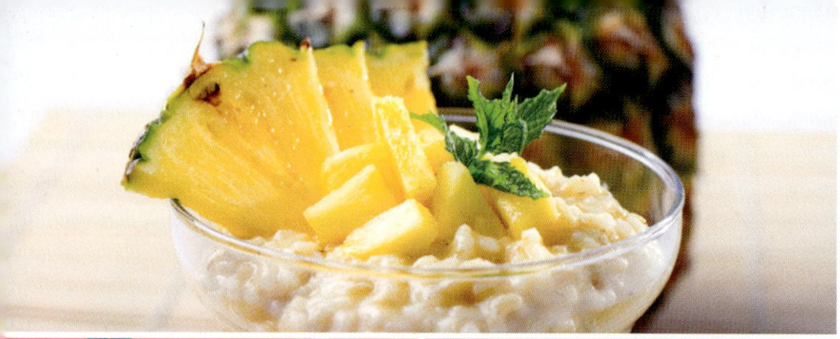
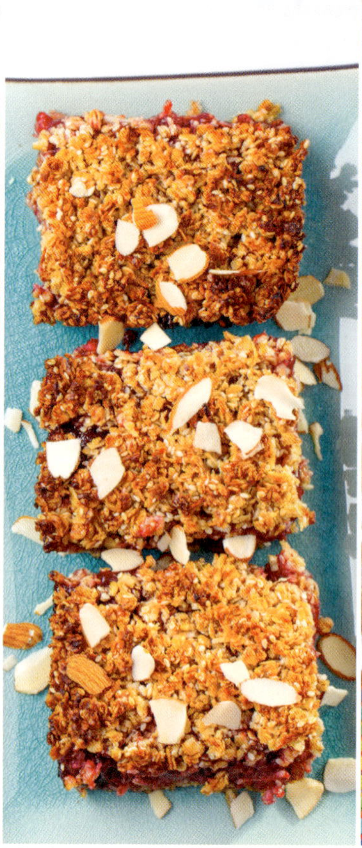
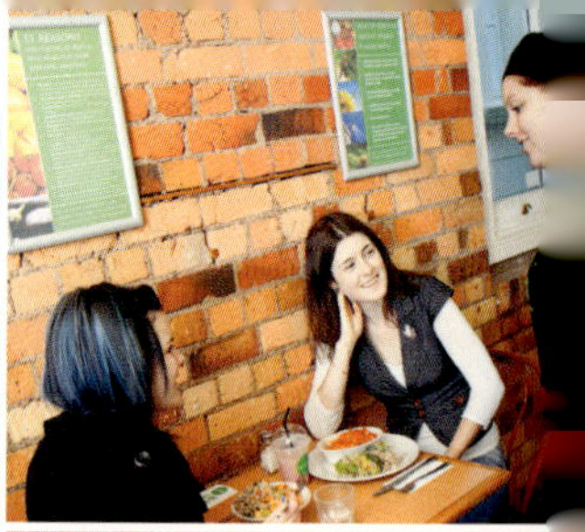
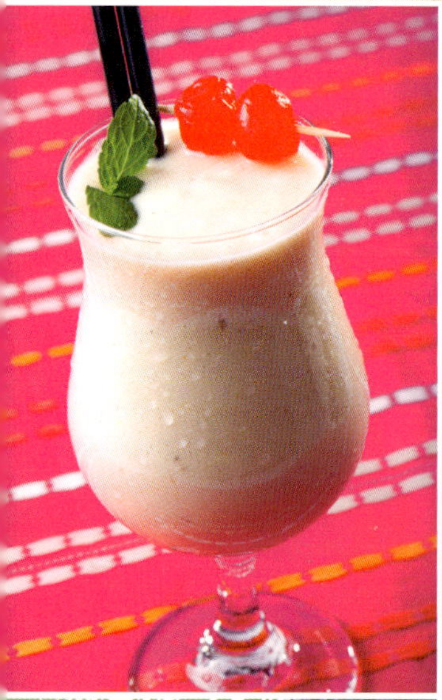
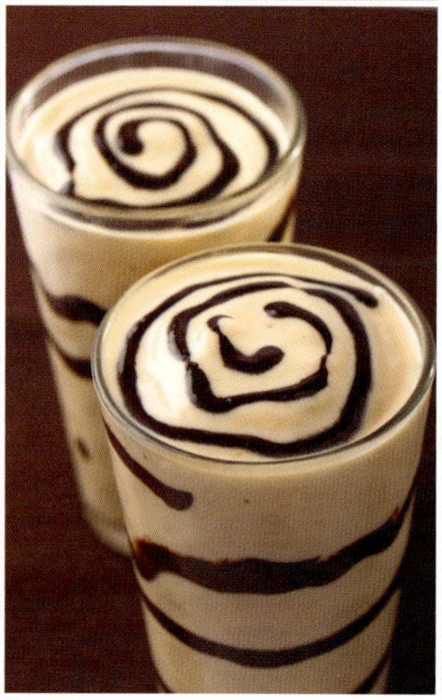
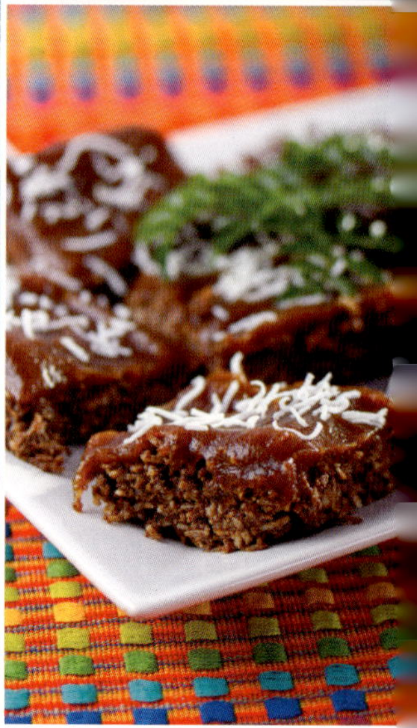
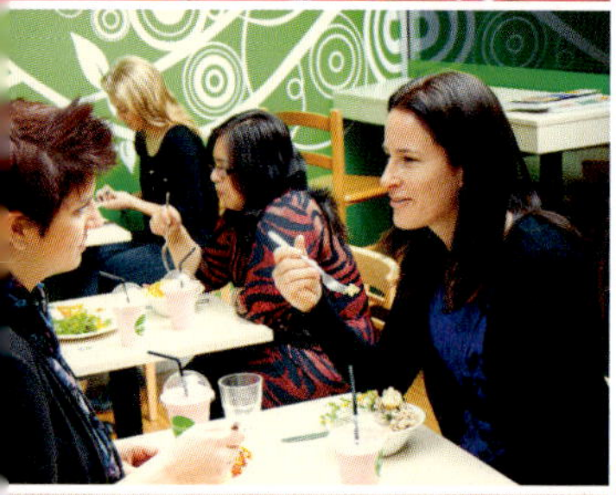
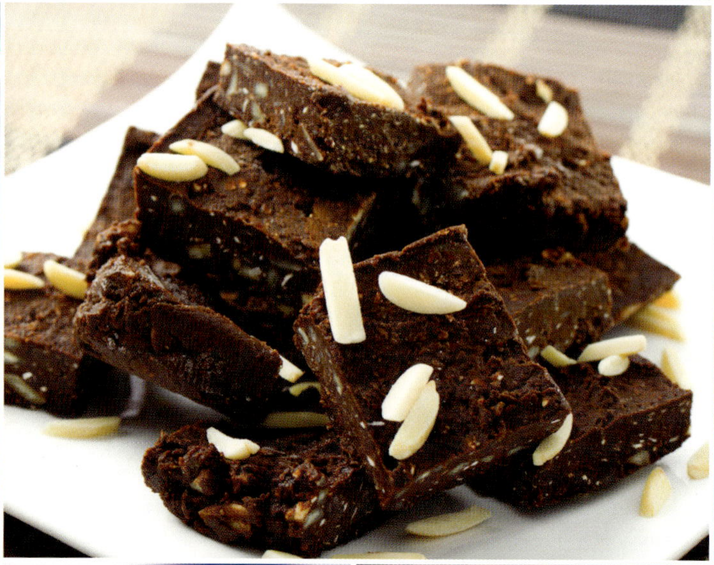
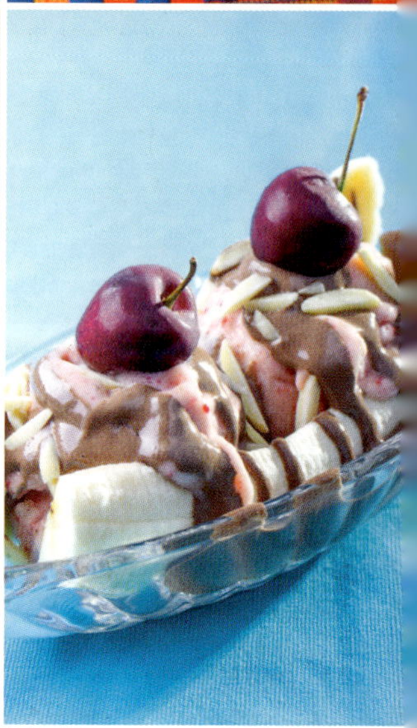
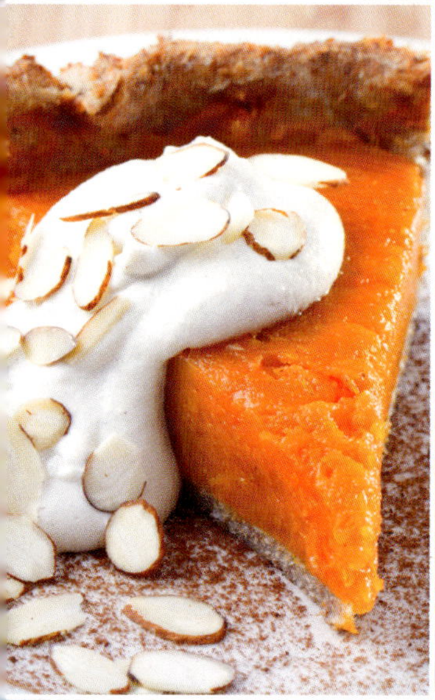
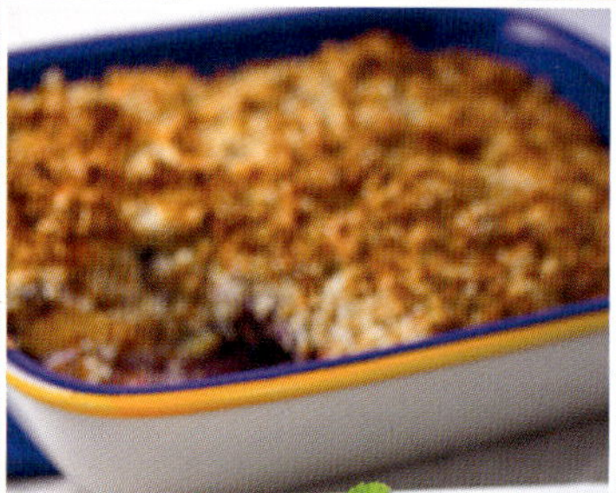
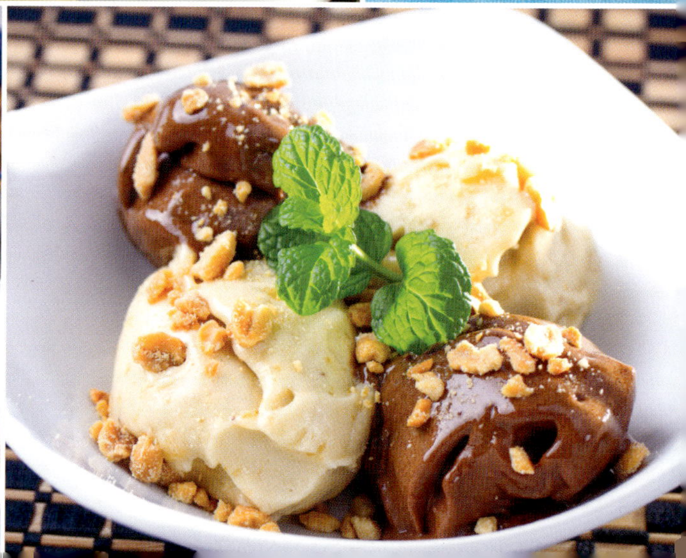
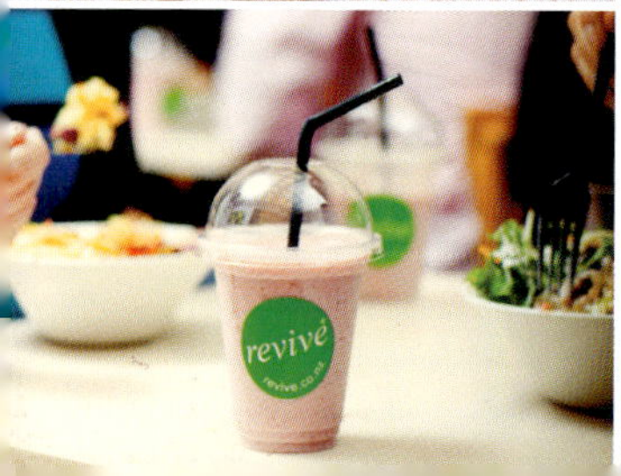
revive
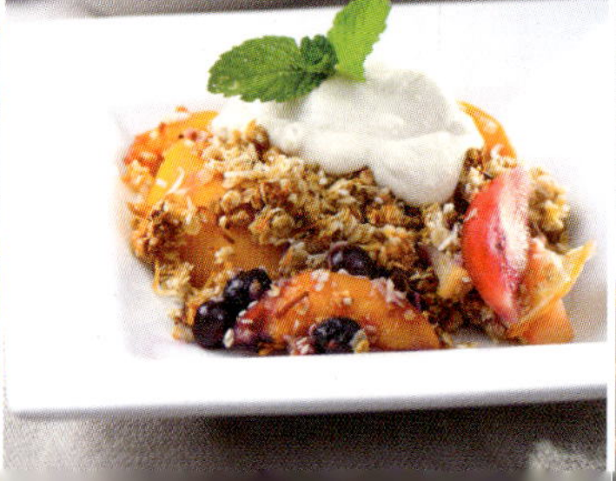

Sweet Things

Plum & Ginger Slice 154

Apricot Bliss Balls 156

Better Than Ice Cream 158

Pineapple Rice Pudding 160

Black Almond Fudge 162

Peanut Butter Smoothie 164

Blueberry, Apple & Peach Crumble 166

Pumpkin Pie 168

Honest Pina Colada 170

Banana Split 172

Coconut & Date Fudge 174

Plum & Ginger Slice

MAKES 8 LARGE SLABS OR 16 SMALL SLABS

3 cups fine rolled oats

½ cup almonds ground

½ cup sesame seeds

½ cup shredded coconut

4 tablespoons oil

¾ cup honey

2 teaspoons ginger puree or finely chopped ginger

1 teaspoon vanilla essence

2 x 800g (25oz) can black plums – drained and stones removed (about 3 cups/ 12 plums)

garnish: sliced almonds

1. Mix all dry ingredients together in a large mixing bowl.
2. Add the oil, honey, ginger and vanilla and mix well.
3. Select a baking tray approximately 20x30cm (8x12in) and brush lightly with oil.
4. Firmly press half the mixture into the baking tray.
5. Drain the plums well and take out any stones. Crush with your fingers, place on top of the oat base and press down.
6. Sprinkle the remaining oat mix evenly on top of the plums and press down evenly. Spray or brush a little oil on top to prevent it burning.
7. Bake for 25 minutes at 180°C (350°F) or until golden brown.
8. Cool and cut into slabs with a serrated knife.
9. Garnish with sliced almonds.

Make sure you press the oat mixture firmly into the tray so it is not crumbly.

The slice may be crumbly when first cooked, however it will firm up after it has cooled.

Sliced Almonds

These crunchy pieces make great ingredients and garnishes. They give a good mouth texture to any dish and look fantastic. If possible get sliced almonds with the brown skins as these give a better contrast.

SWEET THINGS 155

We used to spend hours making these at Revive until I teamed up with Phil an engineer friend of mine who built a machine to make them. We now have a small company that makes, packages and supplies them to Revive and hundreds of other stores in New Zealand. Our product is called "Frooze Balls".

Apricot Bliss Balls

MAKES 26 BALLS

1 cup dried apricots

1 cup dried dates

3 cups boiling water

½ cup almonds

½ cup cashew nuts

¼ cup walnuts

¼ cup sunflower seeds

garnish: ½ cup white sesame seeds

1. Put the fruit and boiling water in a bowl for 5 minutes to soften. Drain.

2. Combine all fruit, nuts and seeds in a food processor and blend until it forms a big ball.

3. Form into smaller balls and roll in the sesame seeds.

Dried Apricots

Dried apricots usually come in 2 varieties. Either flat half ones, or thick plump whole ones. The thicker ones are generally sweeter and the flat ones tangier. I always use the thick sweeter ones, however some people prefer the tangy, stronger apricot taste.

SWEET THINGS 157

MAKES 2-3 SERVINGS

2 ripe bananas frozen

2 tablespoons runny honey or date puree

ADD FOR VANILLA:

1 teaspoon vanilla essence

ADD FOR CHOCOLATE:

2 tablespoons carob powder

ADD FOR NUTTY:

2 tablespoons peanut or almond butter

ADD FOR BERRY:

½ cup frozen boysenberries, strawberries, blueberries or blackberries

ADD FOR MANGO:

1 cup frozen mango chunks

GARNISH IDEAS:

chopped roasted peanuts, almonds or cashew nuts

fresh mint

fresh berries

This recipe was suggested by my friend and photographer Elesha. She said just whizz up a banana in a food processor and you have healthy ice cream. I did not believe her so I gave it a go ... and it worked! Just a banana on its own tastes great. But I couldn't help adding more flavours so there are some other options included here!

Better Than Ice Cream

1. Take the skin off your bananas and break into small cubes. Freeze overnight (at least 8 hours).

2. Put banana, honey if desired, and your flavour option in an s-blade style food processor and blend. It will start off becoming flaky and clumpy. After around 1 minute it should start to combine and all of a sudden it will develop a creamy texture.

3. Sometimes the mixture sticks so it avoids the blades. Either chop the pieces smaller or stop the machine and push the lumps down into the blades. A couple of tablespoons of water can assist however too much will make the mixture runny so add carefully.

4. Serve immediately.

This recipe will not work in a liquidiser style blender or with a stick blender.

If your bananas are really ripe you may not need to add honey. If they are slightly unripe you may need to add more honey.

You can store this in the freezer for 10-20 minutes before serving, however if you store longer than this it just becomes a solid block.

Frozen Bananas

A little time putting bananas in your freezer will open up a whole new delicious world of smoothies and healthy ice creams. Make sure you remove the skin and break into small sections to make it easier on your food processor. Bananas generally need overnight to freeze, not just a couple of hours.

SWEET THINGS 159

This is a nice breakfast or healthy dessert treat! Very simple ingredients.

Pineapple Rice Pudding

MAKES 4 X 1 CUP SERVES

1 cup short grain brown rice

1 cup boiling water

1 cup rice or almond milk

2 frozen bananas

½ fresh pineapple peeled and roughly diced

1. Simmer rice, water and milk for 30-40 minutes in a pot (lid on) at low heat or until cooked and soft.
2. In a blender, blend the banana and ¼ of the pineapple.
3. Combine banana/pineapple mix and rice together.
4. Chop the remaining pineapple into small cubes.
5. Serve and garnish with the chopped pineapple.

Optional: add ½ cup coconut cream for a creamier mixture.

Optional: add a pinch of cinnamon or a couple of drops of vanilla essence.

Short Grain Brown Rice

I usually use long grain brown rice when serving with curries as it is easier to chew. However short grain is great for salads and anytime you want a creamy and chewier style rice. It does take a little longer to cook than long grain rice.

SWEET THINGS 161

Who would have thought that black beans could be used in a sweet treat? They produce a nice fudge-like texture in this fudge that doesn't contain chocolate, processed sugar or butter! The only small catch is that you have to serve just out of the freezer or it goes quite soft.

Black Almond Fudge

MAKES 12 PIECES

- 1 cup dates
- 1 cup boiling water
- 1 x 400g can (2 cups) black beans
- 1 ripe banana
- ½ cup carob powder
- ½ cup rolled oats
- ½ cup ground almonds
- 2 teaspoon vanilla
- 4 tablespoons honey
- ½ cup slivered almonds
- optional: 1 teaspoon fresh chilli or chilli flakes

1. Soak the dates in the boiling water for around 5 minutes to soften. Drain.
2. Put all ingredients (except slivered almonds) into a food processor and blend until a thick lump bounces around the machine.
3. Chilli goes well with chocolate so add some if you like a little heat.
4. Add the slivered almonds to the mix but do not blend.
5. Choose a baking tray around 15x25cm (6x10in). Line with baking paper and spoon in the mixture. Flatten out with a spoon.
6. Bake at 180°C (350°F) for 30 minutes.
7. Cut into squares using a sharp knife.

You may need to add more oats or a little water to get the right consistency or if the food processor is having difficulties.

This slice also tastes great when not cooked and just frozen.

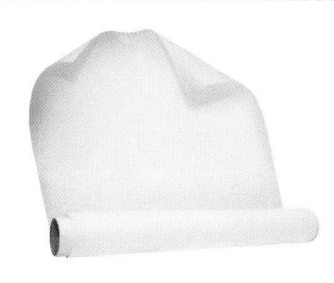

Baking Paper

This is a great way to keep your oven trays clean and keeps things from sticking when roasting or baking. Also you need less oil. Just roll it out before you put the food on.

SWEET THINGS   163

This smoothie is a great light dessert option. With a little decoration it looks awesome too!

Peanut Butter Smoothie

2 X 250ML (8OZ) SERVES

1 large ripe banana frozen

1 tablespoon peanut butter

1 cup soy or almond milk

DECORATION:

¼ cup carob powder

¼ cup water

1. Put banana, peanut butter and milk into a blender and blend until smooth.

2. Mix the carob powder and water into a thick paste. Put into a squirty bottle and decorate the empty glass on the inside.

3. Pour in the smoothie and decorate on top.

SWEET THINGS 165

Blueberry, Apple & Peach Crumble

MAKES 8 X 1 CUP SERVES

6 apples thinly sliced

1 cup boiling water

1 cup frozen blueberries

2 x 400g (12oz) cans peaches drained

TOPPING

1½ cups fine oats

½ cup coconut

½ cup sesame seeds

3 tablespoons oil

½ cup honey

garnish: mint

garnish: cashew cream

1. In a pot cook the apples and water for around 30 minutes or until soft.
2. Layer the apple, peaches and blueberries in a baking dish.
3. In a bowl mix all topping ingredients together.
4. Sprinkle the topping mix on top of fruit pressing down very lightly so you retain the open texture.
5. Bake at 150°C (300°F) for 25 minutes or until golden brown.
6. Serve with cashew cream.

Canned Peaches

These are a great sweet fruit to have in the cupboard. Buy the cans in "natural juice" rather than "syrup" as they will have less sugars and be better for you.

SWEET THINGS 167

I recently visited the United States and was stunned to find that you could not just buy pumpkin from the supermarket as it was a very seasonal item and they usually sell in a can. However butternut was freely available and a good substitute.

Pumpkin Pie

MAKES 8 SERVES

PASTRY

1¾ cups wholemeal flour

½ cup almonds or other nuts

4 tablespoons oil

¼ teaspoon salt

1 cup water

oil for brushing

FILLING

5 cups pumpkin or butternut roasted so it is very soft

2 tablespoons honey or date puree

¼ teaspoon salt

½ teaspoon nutmeg

¼ teaspoon cinnamon

½ teaspoon finely chopped ginger or ginger puree

2 teaspoons arrowroot or cornflour

2 tablespoons water

garnish: almonds sliced

garnish: cashew cream

1. Put pastry ingredients into a food processor and blend until it forms a ball. You may have to add a little more flour.

2. On a floured bench or board, use a rolling pin to roll out the pastry into an area big enough to cover your dish and sides.

3. Carefully place into an oiled round pie dish and press up the sides. Trim off excess and lightly brush oil on the base.

4. Cook the pastry in the oven for 10 minutes at 180°C (350°F).

5. Mix the arrowroot and water in a cup and combine with all other filling ingredients in your food processor. Blend until smooth.

6. Spoon filling into the half cooked pastry shell and bake for another 20 minutes at 180°C (350°F).

7. Chill for at least an hour. Cut into wedges and serve with cashew cream and sliced almonds as a garnish.

You can dust your plate with carob powder before serving for extra effect.

If you do not have a food processor you can still make this recipe, you just need to do more elbow work mixing and mashing.

SWEET THINGS 169

Honest Pina Colada

MAKES 3 X 1 CUP SERVES

2 bananas (frozen if possible)

450g (14oz) can pineapple (drain and reserve juice)

½ cup coconut cream

1. Put all ingredients into a blender (or use a stick blender) and blend until smooth.

2. Add back any pineapple juice and blend to achieve the consistency you like.

3. Serve immediately.

If you use non-frozen bananas, put them and the pineapple in the refrigerator before you blend so you have a cold drink.

You can use chunks, crushed or rings if using canned pineapple. If you have fresh pineapple it will also work well.

SWEET THINGS 171

Yes you can have delicious desserts without all the fat, dairy and processed sugars. Try this recipe, children will love it!

Banana Split

MAKES 2 SERVES

2 large ripe bananas

NATURAL ICE CREAM

½ cup frozen strawberries

1 large frozen banana diced

1 tablespoon honey

SAUCE

2 teaspoons carob powder

¼ cup cashew nuts

¼ cup water

GARNISHES

cherries

slivered almonds

1. Split the bananas in half and put in your serving dish.

2. In a food processor, blend the "ice cream" ingredients until smooth. You may need to add a little water to help the process. Scoop onto the banana.

3. Blend the sauce ingredients with a blender or stick blender. Drizzle over the natural ice cream.

4. Add garnishes to complete the Banana Split!

The healthy ice cream will melt quickly so you need to work fast for this recipe.

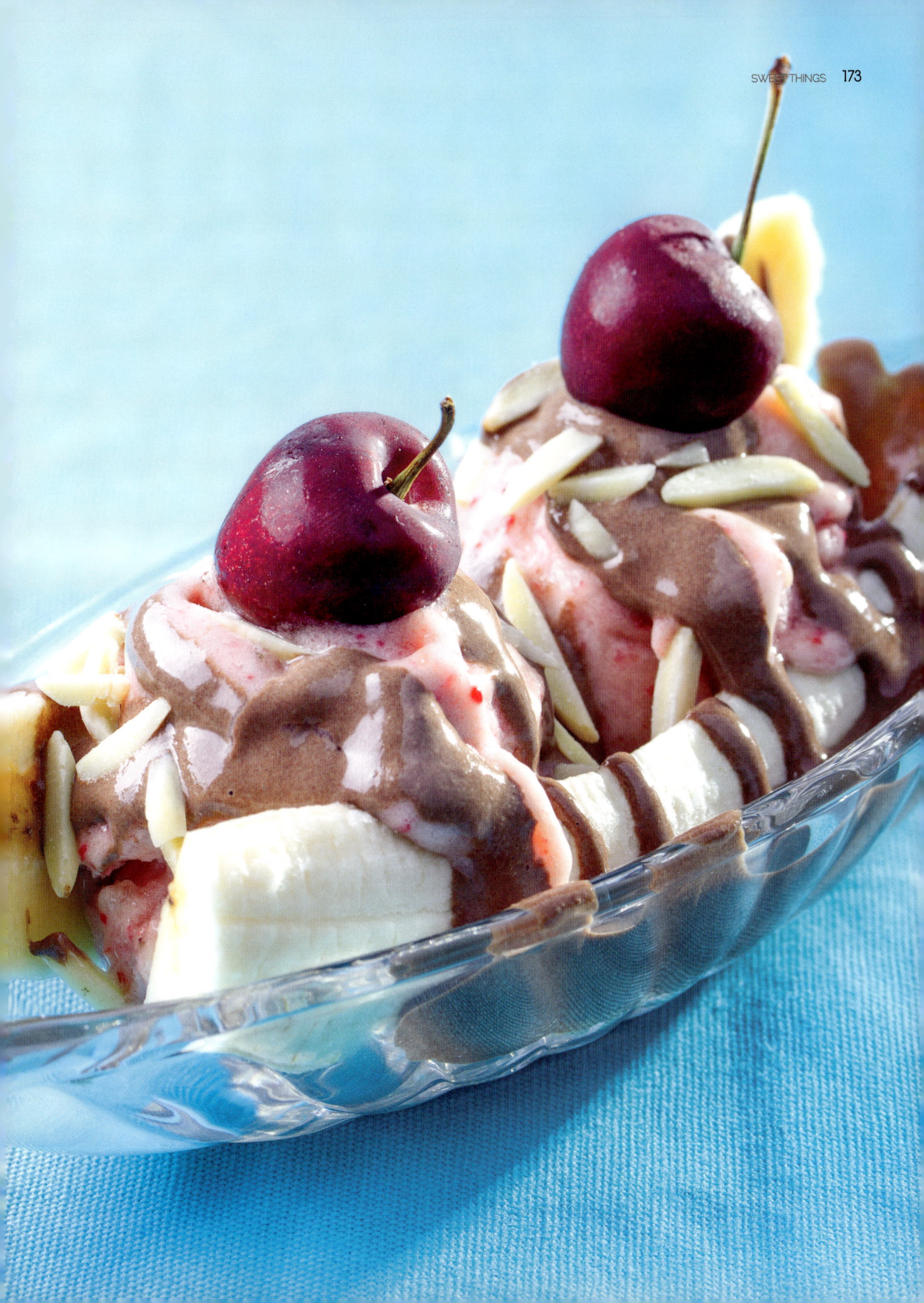

Whenever I ask people what they would like to see in a future recipe book they usually say "more healthy sweets". This is quite challenging as most sweet things people are used to contain copious amounts of sugar, processed flour, butter and often chocolate. This is a great delicious fudge. By keeping in the freezer there is no need for the processed flours and fats that many similar recipes require.

Coconut & Date Fudge

MAKES 16 SLICES

½ cup raw cashew nuts

½ cup raw almonds

1 cup dates

1 cup water

4 tablespoons carob powder

1 cup shredded coconut

TOPPING

1 cup dates

¾ cup boiling water

1. In a food processor blend the nuts, dates, water and carob powder until it clumps together and is fully mixed through.
2. Mix in the coconut.
3. Press into a slice tin.
4. Put the dates and water in a blender or use a stick blender. Let them soak for around 2 minutes to soften and then blend.
5. Spoon over as the topping.
6. Freeze for 2 hours.
7. Cut with a sharp knife and serve immediately.

This dish will need to be stored in the freezer and brought out just before serving.

Carob powder is a healthier alternative to cocoa powder and is available at most health and whole food stores.

You can use any nut combinations you like for this recipe.

SWEET THINGS 175

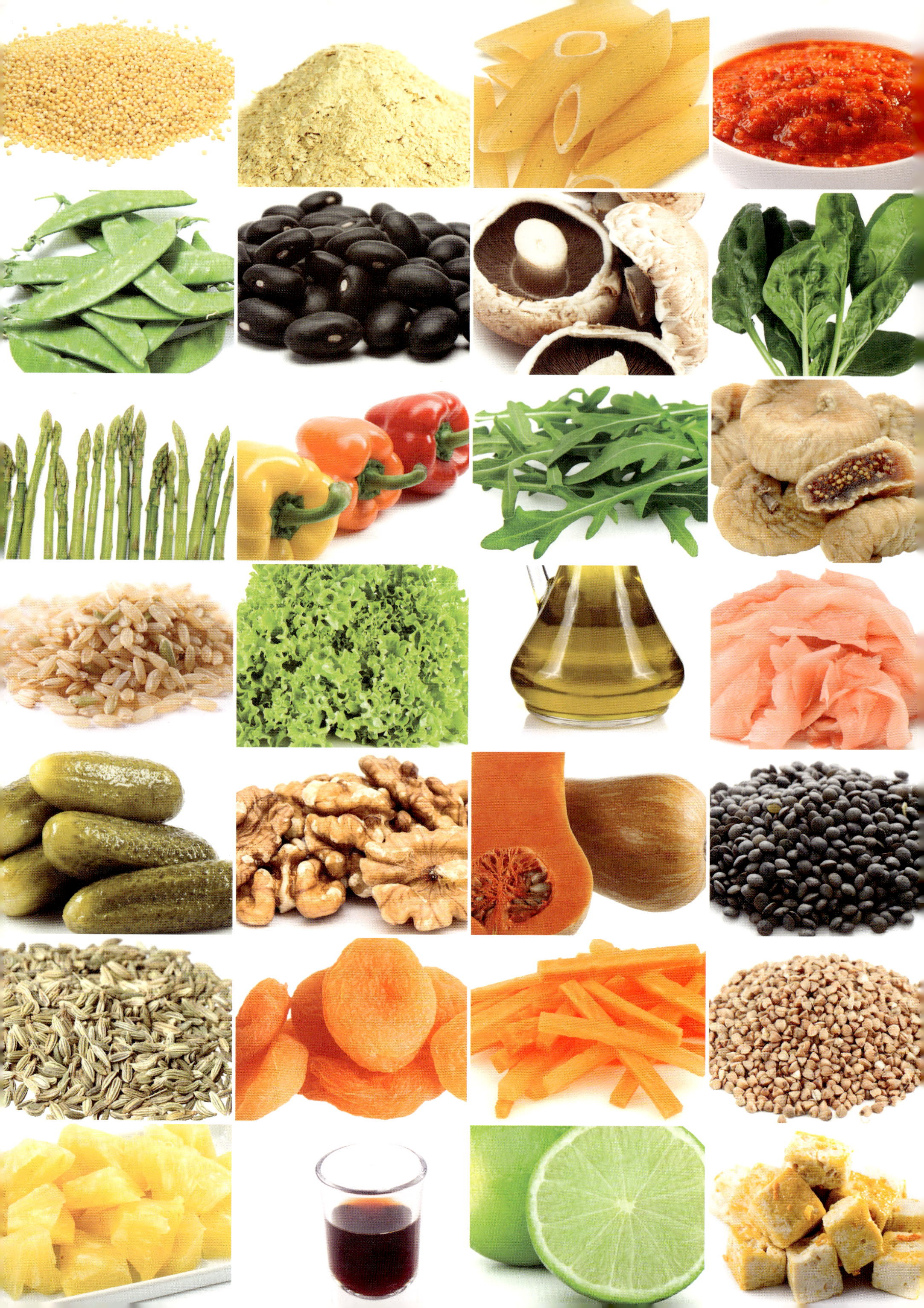

Step-by-Step

Stuffed Veges 178
Dressings 180
Wraps 182
Noodles 184
Pizzas 186

Use this step-by-step guide to help you customise your own recipes. Simply follow the instructions to create dishes based on your favourite ingredients and the ingredients you have available at the time.

Please note you will need a little cooking intelligence to make these work and the suggested serving sizes are a very rough guide. But give them a go and your cooking skills will quickly improve.

For other step-by-step guides see my first 2 books:

The Revive Cafe Cookbook
- Curries
- Smoothies
- Salads
- Stir Fries
- Fritters

The Revive Cafe Cookbook 2
- Soups
- Breakfasts
- Frittatas
- Dips
- Lasagnes

Step-by-Step Stuffed Veges

Choose your favourite vegetable, cook and mix the inside flesh with great flavours and you have a delicious meal!

The quantities in this recipe will vary dramatically depending on the size of your vegetables so adjust accordingly.

ROUGH GUIDE: Makes 6 serves.

1 Shell
cook the vegetable in the oven and scoop out the flesh into a mixing bowl

2 Grain
add to the mixing bowl

3 Flavour
add to the mixing bowl

---

choose 1: (3 veges halved)
- kumara (sweet potato)
- potato
- eggplant (aubergine)
- small pumpkin or butternut
- capsicum (bell pepper)
- marrow (squash)
- courgette (zucchini)

optional choose 1: (1 cup)
- cooked brown rice (short or long)
- cooked quinoa
- fine rolled oats

optional for moisture if needed:
- ½ cup rice, almond or soy milk

choose 2:
- sauteed onion
- garlic
- smoked paprika
- cumin
- honey or date puree
- almond butter (page 133)
- sweet chilli sauce
- Thai curry paste
- nutritional yeast flakes

add:
- ½-1 teaspoon salt

2,903,040 different combinations

4 Texture
add to the mixing bowl, mix and stuff inside the shell

choose 1: (2 cups)

- canned pineapple
- canned cream corn
- frozen peas
- olives
- sauteed mushrooms
- sauteed celery
- diced dates or apricots
- steamed broccoli (small florets)
- black beans
- chickpeas

5 Sprinkle
sprinkle on top then bake for 10-20 minutes at 180°C (350°F)

choose 1: (1 tablespoon)

- white sesame seeds
- black sesame seeds
- chopped peanuts
- sliced almonds
- raw cashew nuts
- poppy seeds

optional:

lightly brush or spray with oil

6 Garnish
sprinkle or drizzle over after cooked

choose 1:

- fresh coriander (cilantro)
- fresh parsley
- basil pesto (page 135)
- cheezy cashew sauce (page 122)
- hummus
- guacamole (blended avocado)

STEP-BY-STEP 179

Step-by-Step Dressings

Dressings can make a salad taste amazing.

Use a blender or stick blender and blend ingredients until smooth. Some will just need to be shaken or stirred. If you are making an oil based dressing, add all other ingredients first, and slowly add the oil while blending.

ROUGH GUIDE: Makes around 1-2 cups.

1 Base
add to blender or shaker

2 Tangy
add to blender or shaker

3 Flavour
add to blender or shaker

---

choose 1 or 2:

- ½ cup soy milk
- ½ cup tahini (sesame seed paste)
- 1-3 tablespoons lemon juice
- 1-3 tablespoons lime juice
- ½ cup raw cashew nuts and ½ cup water

add:
- ½ teaspoon salt (or to taste)

---

choose 1 or 2:

- 2 cloves garlic
- 1 teaspoon seeded mustard
- 1 tablespoon sweet chilli sauce
- 1 tablespoon honey or date puree
- 1 tablespoon ginger puree or chopped ginger
- ½ cup orange juice

---

choose 1:

- pinch cayenne pepper
- 1 teaspoon Thai curry paste
- 1 teaspoon cumin powder
- 1 teaspoon smoked paprika
- 1 tablespoon poppy seeds
- ½ cup coriander (cilantro)
- ½ cup fresh mint
- 1 tablespoon sesame seeds
- 1 tablespoon miso paste
- 2 tablespoons peanut butter
- 1 tablespoon whole-grain mustard

316,800 different combinations

4 Binding
add to blender or shaker

optional choose 1:

up to ½ cup oil (olive, rice bran, grape seed)

1 ripe avocado

1 mango

5 Liquid
add and shake or blend

optional add:

2 cups skinned cucumber

400g (12oz) can chopped tomatoes

½ cup orange juice

optional depending on thickness:

½–1 cup water

6 Check
for saltiness, flavour, sweetness, texture and adjust

Step-by-Step Wraps

A wrap is a great way to have a meal. Fill it with some delicious ingredients.

Some wraps are cold (usually with fresh ingredients) and some are cooked in the oven for around 20 minutes at 180°C (350°F).

ROUGH GUIDE: Makes 4 wraps.

1 Wrap
select your favourite wrap

choose 1:

burrito

tortilla

herb wrap

(preferably wholemeal)

2 Fresh
stack on top of the wrap do not cook if using any of these ingredients

if cold wrap choose 3:

fancy lettuce

tomato

cucumber

capsicum (bell pepper)

sprouts

red onion

grated carrot

3 Protein
stack on top

choose 2: (4 cups total)

fried tofu

refried beans

falafel balls

hummus

bean dip

chickpeas

beans

STEP-BY-STEP   183

4,630,500 different combinations

4 Flavour
stack on top

5 Garnish
roll up, lightly oil, sprinkle on top than heat

6 Sauce
serve with sauce on the side

choose 1:

sauteed onions

cranberries

roasted pumpkin

sauteed capsicum (bell pepper)

basil pesto (page 135)

olives

sauteed cabbage

choose 1:

sesame seeds (white/black)

sliced almonds

cumin seeds

poppy seeds

cayenne pepper

choose 1:

relish

plum chutney

sweet chilli sauce

aioli (page 134)

tofu mayo (page 132)

Step-by-Step Noodles

Combine some healthy noodles with great flavours and you have an awesome meal.

Just keep adding ingredients to your favourite wok or pan!

ROUGH GUIDE: Makes 2-3 large servings.

1 Veges
saute with a little oil in a wok or frying pan until soft

2 Flavour
mix in and heat

3 Sauce
mix in - add more water for a more soup-like dish

---

choose 4: (2 cups)

sliced onion

zucchini (courgettes) sliced

red, orange & yellow capsicum (bell pepper)

carrot matchsticks

roasted pumpkin or butternut

lotus root

bamboo shoots

---

choose 1:

3 tablespoons soy sauce

Thai curry paste (red, yellow, green, Massaman, Penang)

1 teaspoon curry powder

1 tablespoon ginger puree or chopped ginger

add:

½-1 teaspoon salt

---

choose 1: (1 cup)

satay sauce

miso soup

cold water mixed with 1 tablespoon arrowroot or cornflour

coconut cream or milk

2,419,200 *different combinations*

4 Protein
mix in

5 Noodles
cook according to packet directions in a separate pot, drain and add

6 Garnish
spread over base

---

choose 1: (1 cup)

sauteed tofu

sauteed chickpeas

cooked red lentils

beans (red, black, white)

---

optional: choose 1 or more:

flat rice noodles (many different widths available)

buckwheat noodles

wholemeal spaghetti

vermicelli (round rice noodles)

udon noodles

---

choose 1: (½ cup)

fresh mint

coriander (cilantro)

spring onions (scallions)

lime or lemon wedges

chopped peanuts

roasted cashew nuts

sliced almonds

sliced Asian green vegetables

snow peas

Step-by-Step Pizzas

Making healthy pizzas is easy - just use a good base and load it with great toppings.

Prepare the base and add ingredients.
I like my ingredients chunky but you can prepare them finer if you like it more like a bought pizza.

ROUGH GUIDE: Makes 1 large pizza to serve 4-6 people.

1 Base
prepare

2 Sauce
spread over base

choose 1:

chick bread (page 98)

polenta

wholemeal wheat flour base

pita bread

wrap bread

choose your shape:

large round size

large rectangle size

small mini round size

choose 1: (1-2 cups)

Italian tomato sauce (page 134)

basil pesto (page 135)

cheezy cashew sauce (page 122)

4,465,125 *different combinations*

3 Toppings
add and if required, grill briefly to heat up

4 Fresh
add to pizza

5 Garnish
sprinkle on top

choose 2: (2-3 cups)
- sauteed portobello mushrooms
- sauteed red onion
- sauteed tofu cubes or strips
- roasted pumpkin
- steamed broccoli
- grilled eggplant (aubergine)
- canned red chilli beans

choose 1 or 2: (1 cup)
- sliced or diced capsicum (bell pepper)
- pineapple chunks
- baby spinach
- cherry tomatoes
- rocket or other greens

choose 1 or 2:
- coriander (cilantro)
- olives
- sweet chilli sauce
- cheezy cashew sauce (page 122)
- chopped peanuts
- slivered almonds
- capers
- dollup of hummus (page 124)
- pickled gherkins

Cookbook Series Reference Guide

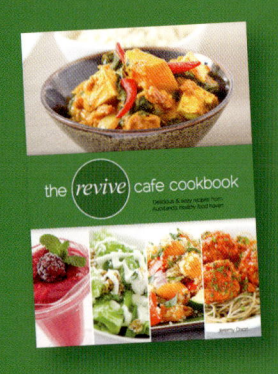

The Revive Cafe Cookbook

STEP BY STEP GUIDES: Curries, Smoothies, Salads, Stir Fries, Fritters

Salads
- Cos Caesar 26
- Moroccan Chickpeas 28
- Seedy Slaw 30
- Classic Greek Salad 32
- Sweet Chilli Roast Veges 34
- Mushroom Risotto Salad 36
- Balsamic Lentil & Roasted Beetroot 38
- Italian Chickpeas 40
- Dukkah Roasted Potatoes 42
- Sweet Bean Medley 44
- Thai Green Curry Veges 46
- Corn & Pepper Fiesta 48
- Chewy Indonesian Rice 50
- Thai Satay Kumara Noodles 52
- Honey Mustard Roasted Potatoes 54
- Moroccan Leek Rice 56
- Almond Carrot Crunch 58
- Satay Cauliflower with Peanuts 60
- Spring Kumara Mingle 62
- Tuscan Mesclun 64
- Revive-dorf Salad 66
- Pacifika Coleslaw 68

Hotpots & Stir Fries
- Pumpkin, Spinach, Ginger & Tofu Curry 72
- Not Butter Chicken 74
- Corn & Potato Chowder 76
- Indonesian Chickpea Satay 78
- Thai Red Curry with Tofu 80
- Dahl Makhani 82
- Dahl-a-touille 84
- Malai Kofta 86
- Mushroom Bhaji 88
- Spanish Bean Stew 90

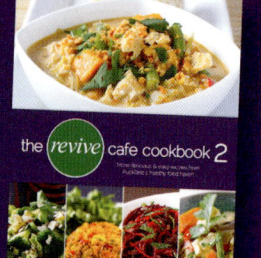

The Revive Cafe Cookbook 2

STEP BY STEP GUIDES: Soups, Breakfasts, Frittatas, Dips, Lasagnes

Salads
- 4C Salad 18
- Sesame Asian Greens 20
- Spiced Date Pilau 22
- Revive Raw Salad 24
- Cos & Courgette Mingle 26
- Thai Satay Noodles 28
- Israeli Couscous 30
- Creamy Roasted Veges 32
- Smoked Spanish Rice 34
- Egyptian Rice & Lentils 36
- Thai Bean Mingle 38
- Pad Thai Noodle Salad 40
- Bombay Roasted Potatoes 42
- Mesclun Mango 44
- Italian Fusilli Mingle 46
- Green Salad & Almonds 48
- Summer Quinoa Mingle 50
- Pesto Infused Roasted Potatoes 52
- Wild Green Salad 54
- Greek Chickpeas 56
- Italian Pumpkin Risotto 58
- Kumara & Cranberry Mingle 60
- Curried Black-Eyed Bean Salad 62
- Baghdad Bulghur 64
- Pesto Penne Pasta 66
- Creamy Thai Rice Salad 68
- Brussels Sprout Medley 70

Hotpots & Stir Fries
- Indonesian Sadur Lodeh 74
- Classic Chickpea Ratatouille 76
- Thai Tofu Green Curry 78
- Not Chicken Alfredo 80
- Mixed Bean Jumbalaya 82

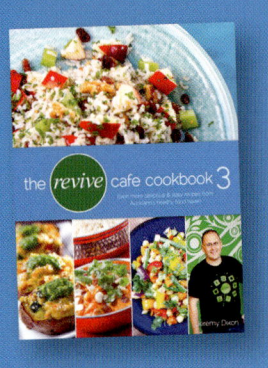

The Revive Cafe Cookbook 3

STEP BY STEP GUIDES: Stuffed Veges, Dressings, Wraps, Noodles, Pizzas

Salads
- Brown Rice Waldorf 16
- Thai Ginger Slaw 18
- Mega Cos Salad 20
- Asian Ginger & Tofu Salad 22
- Autumn Cauliflower Mingle 24
- Blissful Sprout Medley 26
- Rainbow Chickpeas 28
- French Peanut Puy Lentils 30
- Olivier, The Russian Salad 32
- Sweet Shanghai Soy Beans 34
- Tangy Leafy Salad 36
- Italian Risotto 38
- Apple Poppy Coleslaw 40
- Caraway Kumara & Cabbage Salad 42
- Basil Linguine Salad 44
- Indian Curried Cauliflower & Chickpeas 46
- Fragrant Thai Peanut Noodles 48
- Quinoa & Cashew Mingle 50

Hotpots & Stir Fries
- Palak Paneer 54
- Penne Alfredo 56
- Thai Yellow Curry 58
- Peanutty Pineapple Quinoa 60
- Sweet & Sour Tofu 62
- Thai Massaman Lentil Casserole 64
- Cauliflower & Chickpea Satay 66
- Navratan Korma 68
- Mediterranean Quinoa & Sauce 70
- Italian Butter Bean Pasta 72
- Asparagus & Quinoa Stir Fry 74
- Steam Fried Veges 76
- Donburi 78

Revive Chilli 92
Mushroom Goulash 94
Curried Cabbage Stir Fry 96
Kidney Bean Stir Fry 98
Quinoa Stir Fry 100
Miso Bean Mingle 102
Super Nachos 104

Main Meals

Meatless Meatballs 108
Not Chicken Burritos 110
Baked Potato with Chickpea Korma 112
Curried Zucchini Fritters 114
Neat Loaf 116
Honey & Soy Tofu Steaks 118
Spanikopita 120
Pumpkin Risotto Cake 122

Pumpkin & Kumara Balls 124
Mushroom Cannelloni 126
Shepherdess Pie 128
Indian Potato & Chickpea Wraps 130
Scrambled Tofu with Mushrooms 132

Soups

Carrot & Coriander Soup 136
Creamy Tomato Soup 138
Creamy Thai Pumpkin Soup 140
Indian Spiced Lentil Soup 142

Flavour Boosters

Sunflower Cream 146
Classic Hummus 147
Pineapple Salsa 148
Almond Dukkah 149

Revive Aioli 150
Chermoula Dressing 151
Satay Sauce 152
Italian Tomato Sauce 153
Date Puree 154
Onion Jam 155

Sweet Things

Boysenberry Nice-Cream 158
Blueberry & Cashew Cheesecake 160
Buckwheat Hotcakes w Pear Cream 162
Apricot Oat Slice 164
Blueberry Smoothie 166
Banana Date Smoothie 167
Boysenberry Rice Pudding 168
5 Grain Breakfast 170
Bircher Muesli 172

Tofu & Quinoa Stir Fry 84
Moroccan Date & Chickpea Dahl 86
Curried Poppy Seed Dahl 88
Indian Spinach & Chickpea Korma 90
Tarka Dahl 92
Hearty Lentil Casserole 94
Chilli Con Tofu 96
Thai Massaman Peanut Curry 98
Thai Green Curry Lentils 100
Italian White Bean Stew 102
Tuscan Brown Lentils 104
Asian Peanut Stir Fry 106
Mediterranean Chickpea Stir Fry 108
Herbed Lentil & Quinoa Stir Fry 110
Indian Rice Pilaf 112

Main Meals

Baked Thai Corn Cakes 116

Tuscan White Bean Wraps 118
Revive Roast Vege Frittata 120
Greek Potato & Feta Cake 122
Thai Tofu Curry Pie 124
Lentil & Vegetable Lasagne 126
Curried Potato Cakes 128
Indian Curried Filo Pie 130
Chickpea Pizza 132
Beefless Burgers 134
Tuscan White Bean Cannelloni 136
Traditional Corn Fritters 138

Flavour Boosters

Healthy Basil Pesto 142
Chick Bread 144
Avocado Guacamole 146
Root-beet Dip 148
Red Pepper Pesto 149

Revive Relish 150
White Cashew Sauce 152
Tomato Salsa 153
Ravishing Red Bean Dip 154

Sweet Things

Bliss Balls 160
Revive Muesli (Granola) 162
Whipped Cashew Cream 164
Classic Strawberry Smoothie 165
Almond Milk 166
Boysenberry Smoothie 168
Tropical Fruit Salad 169
Hot Honey, Lemon & Ginger Soother 170
Porridge (Oatmeal) 172
Mango Smoothie 174
Carob Ice 175
Muesli Smoothie 176

Main Meals

Scrummy Stuffed Sweet Potato 82
Kumara & Carrot Cakes 84
Pumpkin & Cranberry Filo Parcels 86
Okonomiyaki (Japanese Pancake) 88
Vegetable Pakoras 90
Broccoli Infused Flatbread 92
Summer Burger 94
Smoked Stuffed Peppers 96
Pesto & Potato Chickbread Pizza 98
Courgette & Cauliflower Bake 100
Thai Spring Rolls 102

Soups

Mexican Black Bean Soup 108
Vietnamese Pho Noodles 110
Lentil & Beetroot Borscht 112

Broccoli & Dill Soup 114
Lentil & Kumara Soup 116
Leek & Potato Soup 118

Flavour Boosters

Cheezy Cashew Sauce 122
Basil Hummus 124
Nutty Capsicum Dip 124
Sparkling Lime Juice 126
Almost Egg Spread 128
Thai Ginger Dressing 130
Tofu Mayo 132
Almond Butter 133

Breakfasts

Power Oat Breakfast 138
Nearly French Toast 140
Warming Millet Porridge 142

Buckwheat Waffles 144
Butternut Oatmeal 146
Golden Omelette 148
Portobello Mushrooms 150

Sweet Things

Plum & Ginger Slice 154
Apricot Bliss Balls 156
Better Than Ice Cream 158
Pineapple Rice Pudding 160
Black Almond Fudge 162
Peanut Butter Smoothie 164
Blueberry, Apple & Peach Crumble 166
Pumpkin Pie 168
Honest Pina Colada 170
Banana Split 172
Coconut & Date Fudge 174

Recipe Index

A
Aioli, Revive 134
Alfredo, Penne 56
Almond Butter 133
Almond Fudge, Black 162
Almost Egg Spread 128
Apple & Peach Crumble, Blueberry 166
Apple Poppy Coleslaw 40
Apricot Bliss Balls 156
Asian Ginger & Tofu Salad 22
Asparagus & Quinoa Stir Fry 74
Autumn Cauliflower Mingle 24

B
Bake, Courgette & Cauliflower 100
Balls, Apricot Bliss 156
Banana Split 172
Basil Hummus 124
Basil Linguine Salad 44
Basil Pesto 135
Bean Pasta, Italian Butter 72
Bean Soup, Mexican Black 108
Beans, Sweet Shanghai Soy 34
Beetroot Borscht, Lentil 112
Better Than Ice Cream 158
Black Almond Fudge 162
Black Bean Soup, Mexican 108
Bliss Balls, Apricot 156
Blissful Sprout Medley 26
Blueberry, Apple & Peach Crumble 166
Borscht, Lentil & Beetroot 112
Breakfast, Power Oat 138
Broccoli & Dill Soup 114
Broccoli Infused Flatbread 92
Brown Rice Waldorf 16
Buckwheat Waffles 144
Burger, Summer 94
Butter, Almond 133
Butter Bean Pasta, Italian 72
Butternut Oatmeal 146

C
Cabbage Salad, Caraway Kumara 42
Cakes, Kumara & Carrot 84
Capsicum Dip, Nutty 124
Caraway Kumara & Cabbage Salad 42
Carrot Cakes, Kumara 84
Cashew Mingle, Quinoa 50
Cashew Sauce, Cheezy 122
Casserole, Thai Massaman Lentil 64
Cauliflower Bake, Courgette 100
Cauliflower & Chickpea Satay 66
Cauliflower & Chickpeas, Indian 46
Cauliflower Mingle, Autumn 24
Cheezy Cashew Sauce 122
Chickbread Pizza, Pesto & Potato 98
Chickpea Satay, Cauliflower 66
Chickpeas, Indian Curried 46
Chickpeas, Rainbow 28
Coconut & Date Fudge 174
Coleslaw, Apple Poppy 40
Cos Salad, Mega 20
Courgette & Cauliflower Bake 100
Cranberry Filo Parcels, Pumpkin 86
Crumble, Blueberry, Apple & Peach 166
Curried Cauliflower & Chickpeas 46
Curry, Thai Yellow 58

D
Date Fudge, Coconut 174
Date Puree 135
Dill Soup, Broccoli 114
Dip, Nutty Capsicum 124
Donburi 78
Dressing, Thai Ginger 130

E
Egg Spread, Almost 128

F
Filo Parcels, Pumpkin & Cranberry 86
Flatbread, Broccoli Infused 92
Fragrant Thai Peanut Noodles 48
French Peanut Puy Lentils 30
French Toast, Nearly 140
Fudge, Black Almond 162
Fudge, Coconut & Date 174

G
Ginger Dressing, Thai 130
Ginger Slaw, Thai 18
Ginger Slice, Plum 154
Ginger & Tofu Salad, Asian 22
Golden Omelette 148

H
Honest Pina Colada 170
Hummus, Basil 124

I
Ice Cream, Better Than 158
Indian Curried Cauliflower 46
Italian Butter Bean Pasta 72
Italian Risotto 38
Italian Tomato Sauce 134

J
Japanese Pancake, Okonomiyaki 88
Juice, Sparkling Lime 126

K
Korma, Navratan 68
Kumara & Cabbage Salad, Caraway 42
Kumara & Carrot Cakes 84
Kumara Soup, Lentil 116

L
Leafy Salad, Tangy 36
Leek & Potato Soup 118
Lentil & Beetroot Borscht 112
Lentil Casserole, Thai Massaman 64

Lentil & Kumara Soup 116
Lentils, French Peanut Puy 30
Lime Juice, Sparkling 126
Linguine Salad, Basil 44

M

Massaman Lentil Casserole, Thai 64
Mayo, Tofu 132
Mediterranean Quinoa 70
Medley, Blissful Sprout 26
Mega Cos Salad 20
Mexican Black Bean Soup 108
Millet Porridge, Warming 142
Mingle, Autumn Cauliflower 24
Mingle, Quinoa & Cashew 50
Mushrooms, Portobello 150

N

Navratan Korma 68
Nearly French Toast 140
Noodles, Fragrant Thai Peanut 48
Noodles, Vietnamese Pho 110
Nutty Capsicum Dip 124

O

Oat Breakfast, Power 138
Oatmeal, Butternut 146
Okonomiyaki Japanese Pancake 88
Olivier, The Russian Salad 32
Omelette, Golden 148

P

Pakoras, Vegetable 90
Palak Paneer 54
Pancake, Okonomiyaki Japanese 88
Paneer, Palak 54
Parcels, Pumpkin & Cranberry Filo 86
Pasta, Italian Butter Bean 72
Peach Crumble, Blueberry, Apple 166
Peanut Butter Smoothie 164
Peanut Noodles, Fragrant Thai 48
Peanut Puy Lentils, French 30
Peanutty Pineapple Quinoa 60
Penne Alfredo 56
Peppers, Smoked Stuffed 96
Pesto, Basil 135
Pesto & Potato Chickbread Pizza 98
Pho Noodles, Vietnamese 110

Pie, Pumpkin 168
Pina Colada, Honest 170
Pineapple Quinoa, Peanutty 60
Pineapple Rice Pudding 160
Pizza, Pesto & Potato Chickbread 98
Plum & Ginger Slice 154
Poppy Coleslaw, Apple 40
Porridge, Warming Millet 142
Portobello Mushrooms 150
Potato Chickbread Pizza, Pesto 98
Potato Soup, Leek 118
Power Oat Breakfast 138
Pudding, Pineapple Rice 160
Pumpkin & Cranberry Filo Parcels 86
Pumpkin Pie 168
Puree, Date 135
Puy Lentils, French Peanut 30

Q

Quinoa & Cashew Mingle 50
Quinoa, Mediterranean 70
Quinoa, Peanutty Pineapple 60
Quinoa Stir Fry, Asparagus 74

R

Rainbow Chickpeas 28
Revive Aioli 134
Rice Pudding, Pineapple 160
Rice Waldorf, Brown 16
Risotto, Italian 38
Rolls, Thai Spring 102
Russian Salad, Olivier 32

S

Salad, Asian Ginger & Tofu 22
Salad, Basil Linguine 44
Salad, Caraway Kumara & Cabbage 42
Salad, Mega Cos 20
Salad, Olivier The Russian 32
Salad, Tangy Leafy 36
Satay, Cauliflower & Chickpea 66
Sauce, Cheezy Cashew 122
Sauce, Italian Tomato 134
Scrummy Stuffed Sweet Potato 82
Shanghai Soy Beans, Sweet 34
Slaw, Thai Ginger 18
Slice, Plum & Ginger 154
Smoked Stuffed Peppers 96

Smoothie, Peanut Butter 164
Soup, Broccoli & Dill 114
Soup, Leek & Potato 118
Soup, Lentil & Kumara 116
Soup, Mexican Black Bean 108
Sour Tofu, Sweet 62
Soy Beans, Sweet Shanghai 34
Sparkling Lime Juice 126
Split, Banana 172
Spread, Almost Egg 128
Spring Rolls, Thai 102
Sprout Medley, Blissful 26
Steam Fried Veges 76
Stir Fry, Asparagus & Quinoa 74
Stuffed Peppers, Smoked 96
Stuffed Sweet Potato, Scrummy 82
Summer Burger 94
Sweet Potato, Scrummy Stuffed 82
Sweet Shanghai Soy Beans 34
Sweet & Sour Tofu 62

T

Tangy Leafy Salad 36
Thai Ginger Dressing 130
Thai Ginger Slaw 18
Thai Massaman Lentil Casserole 64
Thai Peanut Noodles, Fragrant 48
Thai Spring Rolls 102
Thai Yellow Curry 58
Toast, Nearly French 140
Tofu Mayo 132
Tofu Salad, Asian Ginger 22
Tofu, Sweet & Sour 62
Tomato Sauce, Italian 134

V

Veges, Steam Fried 76
Vegetable Pakoras 90
Vietnamese Pho Noodles 110

W

Waffles, Buckwheat 144
Waldorf, Brown Rice 16
Warming Millet Porridge 142

Y

Yellow Curry, Thai 58

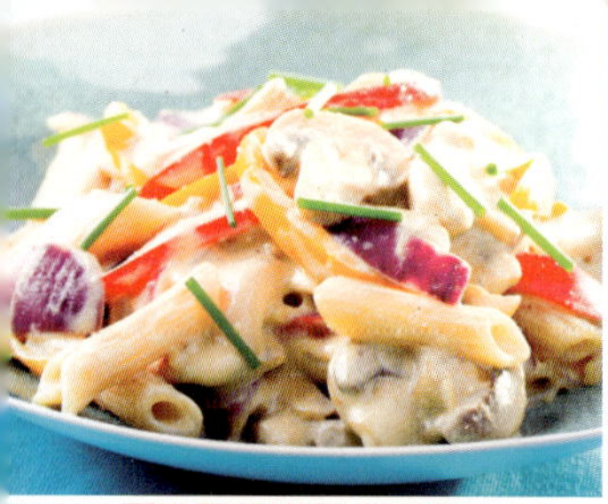
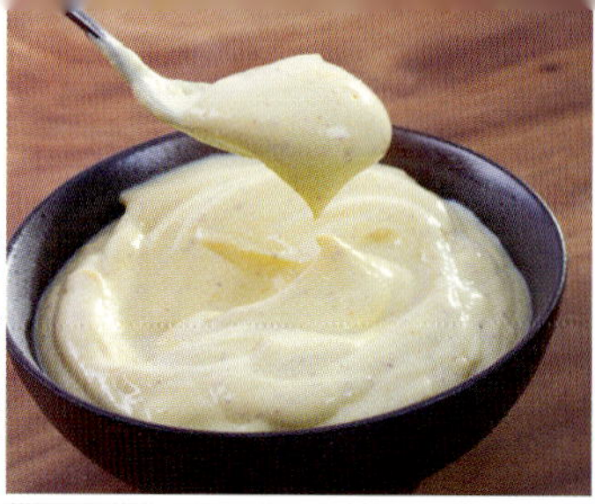
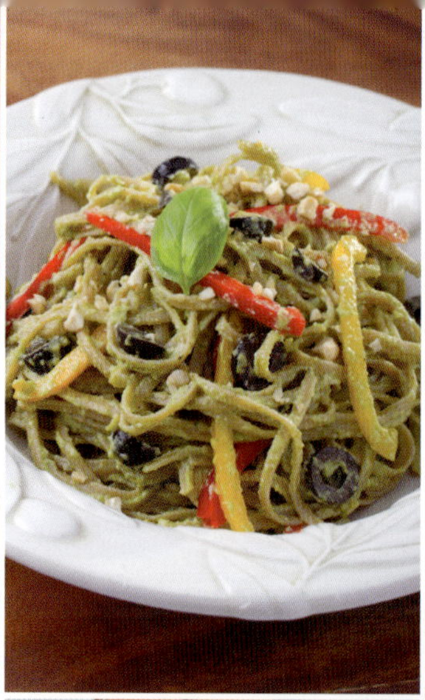
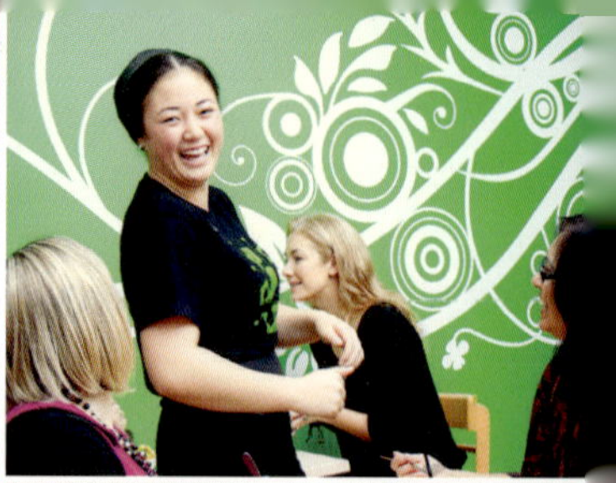
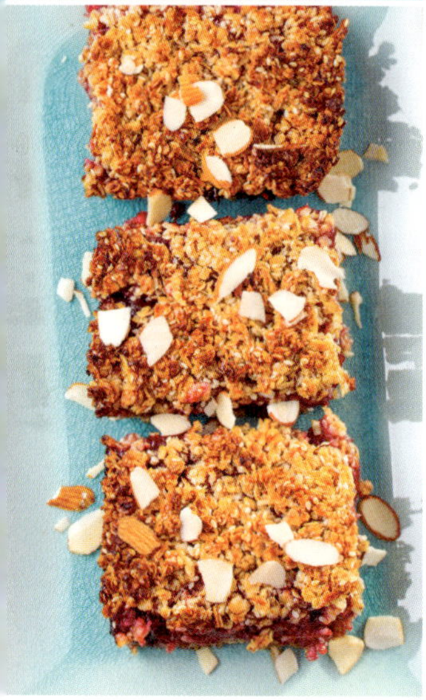
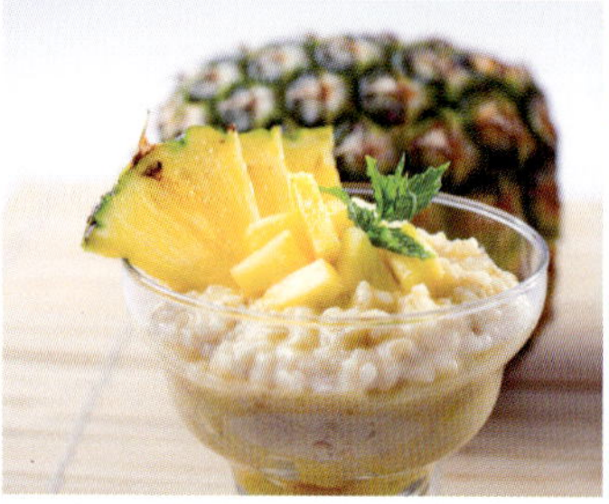
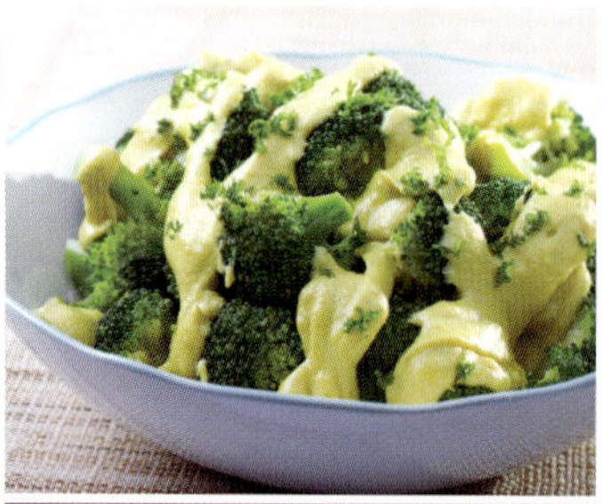
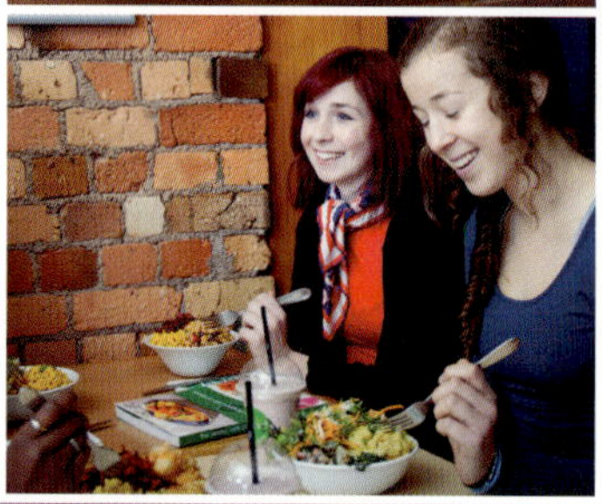
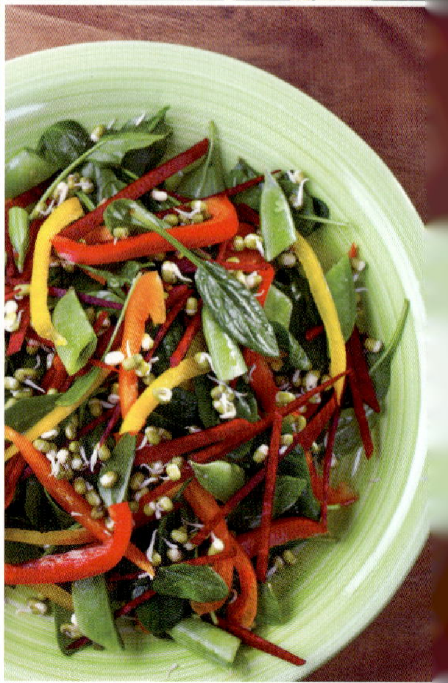
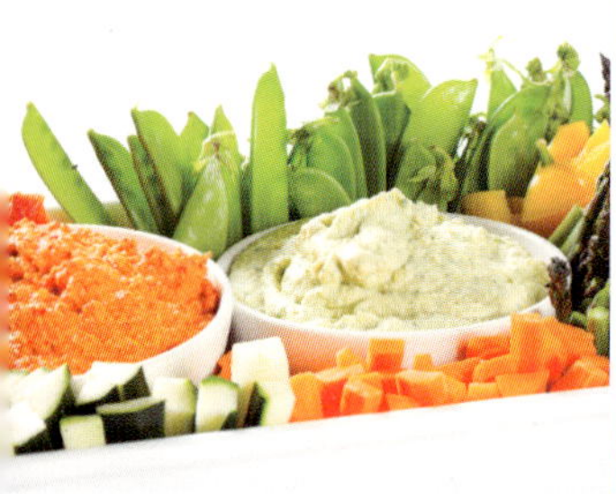
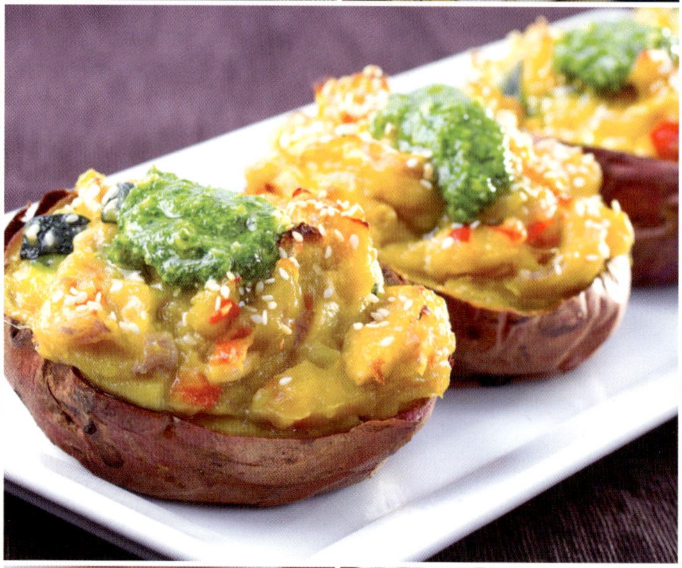
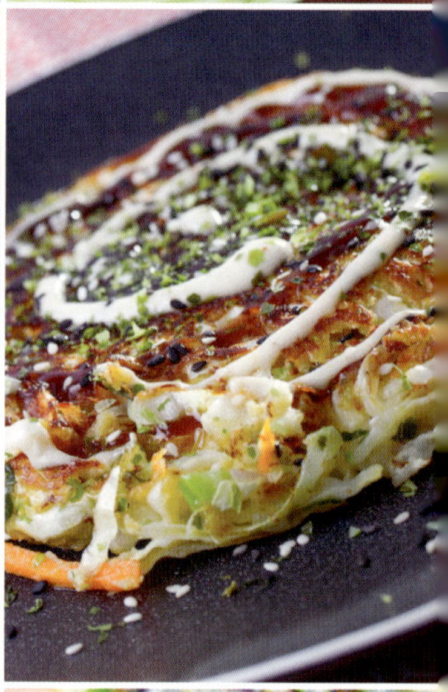
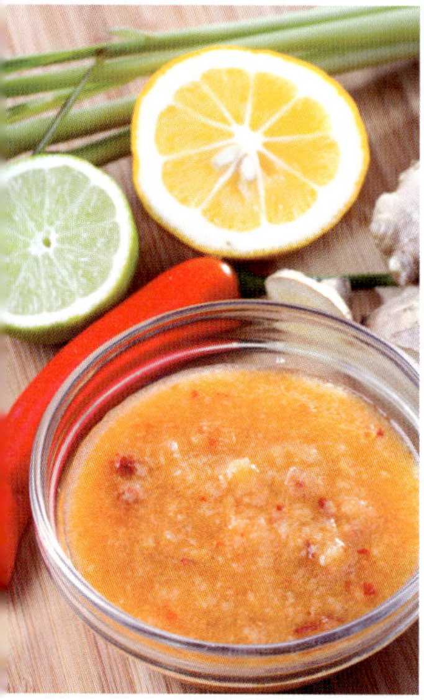
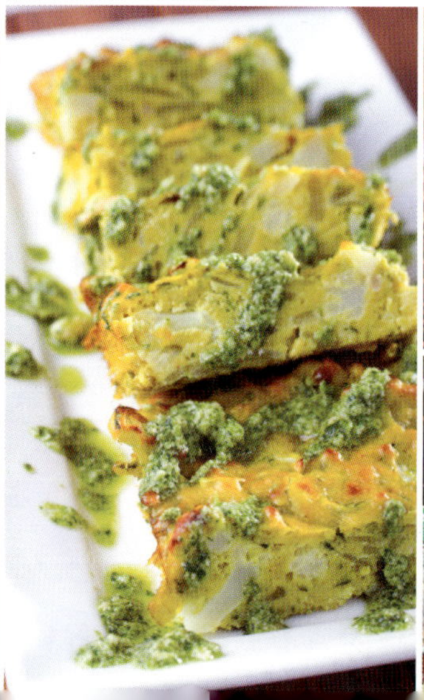
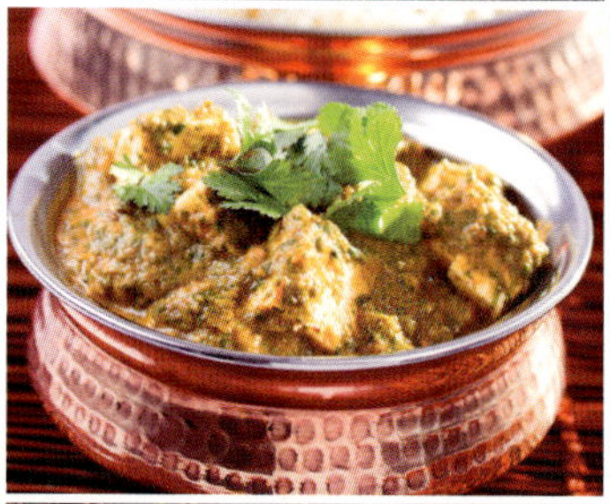
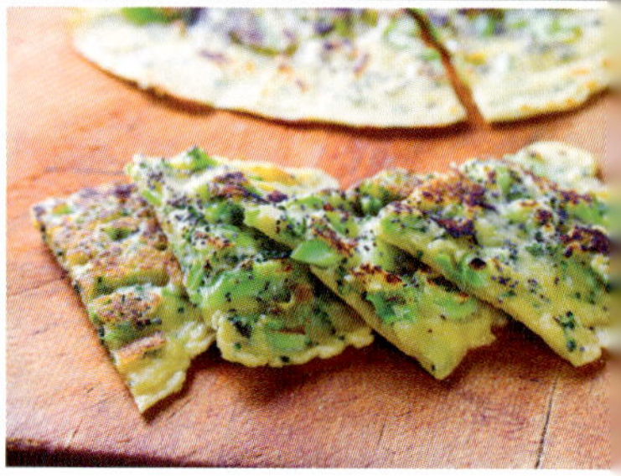
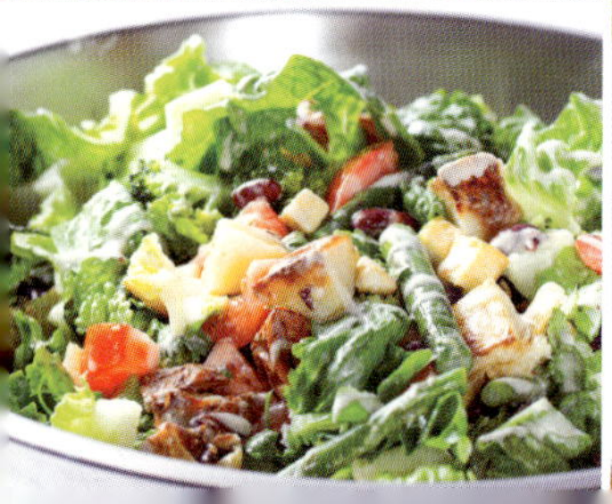
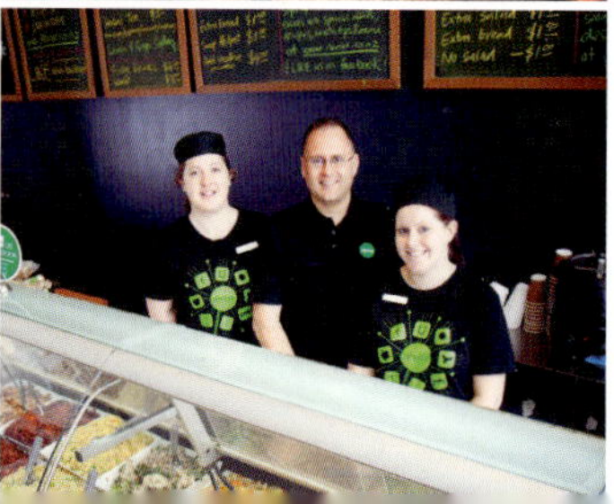
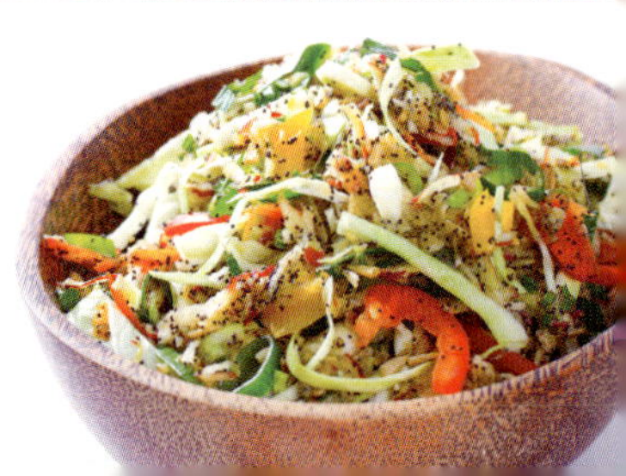